KU-111-003

To James from his brother
Alex. in memory of his visit
to Edinburgh. Aug 1907.

With sincere regards.

Psalms 145 - 18

ONLY FOR JESUS:

MEMORIALS

OF THE LATE

WILLIAM M. MACGREGOR,

MISSIONARY TO CHINA.

BY

LEWIS MUNRO, DINGWALL.

WITH INTRODUCTORY NOTE,

BY

REV. J. H. WILSON, D.D.,

OF THE BARCLAY CHURCH, EDINBURGH.

"ONLY FOR JESUS! . . .
Pulse of all gladness, and nerve of endeavour,
Secret of rest, and the strength of our strife!"
—*F. R. Havergal.*

LONDON: S. W. PARTRIDGE & CO., 9 PATERNOSTER ROW.
DINGWALL: LEWIS MUNRO, ROSS-SHIRE JOURNAL OFFICE.

PREFACE.

THIS little Memoir is published in the belief that, with the blessing of God's Spirit, it is fitted to do good. What is lacking in stirring incident, will, it is hoped, be considered more than compensated for by the whole-hearted consecration and missionary zeal that breathe throughout the life recorded.

It has been attempted, as far as possible, to make the subject of the book relate his own story, and express his own sentiments, the author's duty being mainly that of presenting, in a connected form, the materials at his disposal.

Whatever profits may be realised on this edition will be handed to Mrs. Macgregor, the widowed mother of the young missionary.

DINGWALL, *August, 1888.*

INTRODUCTORY NOTE

BY

REV. J. H. WILSON, D.D.,

BARCLAY CHURCH, EDINBURGH.

I HAVE much pleasure in complying with the request of my friend, Mr Munro, that I should write a few words of preface to this little book, which is possessed of the deepest and most thrilling interest, and I am sure needs only to be known, in order to assert a place for itself among other records of earnest and devoted Christian life and work.

The "Memorials" are necessarily brief, and more or less fragmentary, but they amply suffice to show God's wonderful way of accomplishing His purpose in providence and in grace. It is often remarked that, when the children of godly parents wander out of the way, they go further and more hopelessly astray than others; but this allegation receives an emphatic contradiction in the case before us, which shows the unspeakable value of early Christian training in recovering to faith those who have lost it, and in laying the foundations of high Christian attainment and eminent usefulness in after life. I have read few narratives of the kind which more signally illustrate the grace of God and His faithfulness to His promise.

The deliverance of the young sceptic from the power of unbelief may seem to some to have turned on a very slight circumstance. But it should be borne in mind that that was preceded by an intelligent acquaintance with the Word of God, and by many Christian influences of a helpful kind, so that a very simple occasion, through the Spirit's working, might suffice to turn the tide and bring about a radical change.

The saying—"Every Christian a missionary!" cannot be too often reiterated, or illustrated in too great a variety of instances. It holds good alike in the case of peer and peasant. It is God's call to each of His redeemed people. And the way is equally open to men like Lord Shaftesbury and to the humblest Christian tradesman. It is striking to find a young artizan, in a quiet country town in the north of Scotland, without anything beyond a common school education, after his heart has been touched by the love of Christ, throwing himself into the thick of work in the great world of London, at street corners and under railway arches attacking the very citadel of Satan's kingdom, pressing Christ on the acceptance of the careless and ungodly, and dealing with the clever secularist on his own ground, and then, having his heart drawn out to the heathen world, and ending his days in the service of Christ in China. What he and men like the late Dr. James Henderson of China accomplished, any young Christian peasant or artizan, with the requisite gifts, may aspire to. I am persuaded that some of the Lord's best gifts to His Church, in these days, will be found among those belonging to these classes, largely self-educated perhaps, but men of energy, persistency, and good judgment.

I do not see how we can hope to evangelize the waste places in our large cities at home—far less the hundreds of millions of heathens and Mohammedans and Jews abroad, except by the utilizing, to a far larger extent, of men of the class and stamp of young Macgregor. One service which Mr. Hudson Taylor has done, in connection with the China Inland Mission, apart from the direct work itself, has been to show that, in addition to the indispensable staff of regularly trained missionaries, the door is open to men of strong faith and competent gifts, from every class of society.

The removal of such men, at the very threshold of what seemed a great life-work, is very mysterious. And yet we are not to think of them as having failed, as regards the end to which their lives had been consecrated. It has only been accomplished in a different way. So it was with the beloved Henry Martyn. By the story of his life and labours and early death, Henry Watson Fox of Masulipatam, and others of like spirit, were led to take up the colours that had fallen from the young missionary's hand. So it was with Dr. Alexander Duff's early college friend Urquhart, who had consecrated his life to the service of Christ among the heathen. Urquhart's purpose was unfulfilled, but his early removal called forth in his stead one of the greatest missionaries of modern times. And we can hardly doubt that the simple narrative, which this book contains, of the brief life and scarcely begun missionary labours of WILLIAM MACGREGOR, will fire the hearts of other young men, in his native town and country, and in other lands, to serve themselves heirs to his faith and zeal and burning desire to help on the coming of Christ's Kingdom.

The book is fitly entitled "ONLY FOR JESUS." That furnishes the key to a life that to some may appear inexplicable.

"You are going very far away," said a friend to a young missionary's wife who was leaving for Japan.

"Yes," was the reply, "it would be very far to go, for anything else, but it is not too far to go *for Jesus!*"

The last proof sheets have been sent to me for perusal, while spending an autumn holiday in the Upper Engadine. I cannot well express the deep emotion with which I have read the closing chapter. It is a beautiful story of grace, and one can but pray and hope that in many of our family circles, as in this case, one member after another may be brought into the kingdom of God, till "not a hoof shall be left behind."

J. H. W.

The last pencil sketch [illegible] for the present
while spending [illegible] of the Upper Engadine
[illegible]

CONTENTS.

CHAPTER I.—UNCONVERTED DAYS.

CHAPTER II.—CONVERSION.

CHAPTER III.—UPWARD AND ONWARD.

CHAPTER IV.—THOUGHTS OF BECOMING A MISSIONARY, AND ABOUNDING LABOURS.

CHAPTER I.

UNCONVERTED DAYS.

BIRTH—LEAVING HOME FOR FIRST TIME—APPRENTICESHIP—ITINERANCY—DEATH OF A BROTHER—UNREAL PIETY—KINDNESS TO PARENTS—GOES TO EDINBURGH—BECOMES A SCEPTIC—PROCEEDS TO NEWCASTLE—BECOMES AN ABSTAINER—APPLYING FOR WORK—MIRACULOUS ESCAPE—PROCEEDS TO LONDON—EXTRACTS FROM LETTERS.

WILLIAM MACGREGOR was born of respectable parents, at the now well-known Strathpeffer Spa, Ross-shire, on April 21, 1854, and ended his earthly career at Gan-K'ing, China, on October 29, 1882. The family removed from Strathpeffer, to the neighbouring town of Dingwall, when young Macgregor was in his third year. His early days were passed uneventfully. As a boy he was thoughtful, affectionate, and frolicsome. No special pains were bestowed upon his education, which was received at the Dingwall Free Church School. The circumstances of the family, indeed, required that he should cease attending school at the age of fourteen, and enter upon a life of toil. As a schoolboy he took a spirited part in all the games of the play-ground, was a keen cricketer, and attained the position of "Captain" of the "Greenhill Club." His sense of humour, if mellowed in later life, never left him; and he used to relate, with glee, amusing incidents connected with his early life.

At fourteen years of age, Macgregor was hired to go to Aberdeen to take charge of a gentleman's pony and phaeton. Here he remained for eight months. It was the first occasion on which he left home, and from this time forward, notwithstanding strong family attachments, he scarcely ever knew what it was to live with his friends for any protracted period. On returning from Aberdeen, he began an apprenticeship, as a carpenter, with his father, subsequently entering the employment of another townsman. All who have read Hugh Miller's "Schools and Schoolmasters" know that the occupation of a Highland mason or carpenter involves much hardship and itinerancy. Highland towns are few and small, and employment has to be sought at the numerous country residences, shooting lodges, and farm steadings, and in districts often remotely situated. The conditions of life have vastly improved since Miller's time, but the lot of the Highland workman, who is shifted from country place to country place, is still far from enviable. Macgregor, in following his occupation, had a full share of these changes, and he did not like them.

Still worse, he was all the while a wanderer in the "far country," though it cannot be said that "he wasted his substance with riotous living." Morally, his life was correct and honourable. He was respected by his employer and fellow-workmen as a craftsman of expertness and skill, and a very companionable fellow. As a son and brother he was kind and dutiful—loving and loved. Probably had his course ended at this time his friends would have entertained the hope that his latter end was peace. Not only was his character unblemished, but his letters were not destitute of pious utterances. Strong emotion often makes men evince a piety that is not deep-rooted or abiding. They may not wish to deceive others, but they are themselves deceived. Macgregor's piety of 1882 is as wide apart from that of 1872 as the poles are asunder. Natural feelings make him transiently pious in 1872; Christ Jesus, living and reigning in his heart by faith, makes a wholly-consecrated man of him in 1882.

In December of 1872 his eldest brother, Charles, was smitten down by small-pox, and the already aged father went south to minister to the dying son. The disease ended fatally in a few days, and news of the sad event was sent back to the sorrowing family in Dingwall. William Macgregor, in replying to his father's letter, after telling of the grief experienced at home, writes :—

"We are in such a state we do not know what to do or say. . . . It has been the Lord's will to take our dear one from us. . . . Our desire is to lay his body beside the loved ones who have gone before, if that be possible; but the Lord's will be done. . . . May God bless, guide, and protect you, my dear father."

He could also discuss preachers. Writing on November 10, 1873, to his father, who was then working in the country, he says :—

"The Rev. Mr. Munro, Maryburgh, was buried in Fodderty Churchyard to-day. There is no word of our own minister [Rev. Dr. John Kennedy, then absent on a tour in quest of health in America] coming home yet. We have meanwhile an excellent substitute in Dr. Hugh Martin. I have never heard a finer preacher."

To his mother, about this time, he wrote from the country:—

"I hope the lassies are good and kind to you. You must try to be cheerful. As our dear departed Charlie used to say—

"'What is the use of repining,
For where there's a will there's a way.'

"Father was asking how I liked this place. I hate it. . . . We have had very bad weather for the last week. We have been wet to the skin. . . . Love to Tom.* Tell him I am very proud of his taking two prizes at school. . . . May God bless you all."

Macgregor's obligations to his parents were not discharged with mere expressions of affection. The letter concludes with a postscript, intimating the inclosure of an order on his employer, "for a few pounds." It was thus with him in his unconverted days, and after his conversion there was certainly no change for the worse. In after life, in London, he occasionally experienced what it was to be out of employment. His principal regret at such times was his inability to help

* His youngest brother—a lad of very brilliant parts, who died in London in 1885—and who is frequently referred to in these pages.

his parents, who were now becoming infirm. When his heart, at a later period, became set on devoting his life to missionary work in China, it was the intensity of his zeal for God's service, and the salvation of perishing millions of heathen, together with the consideration that the younger members of the family were growing up, and were likely to bear the family burden, that must have enabled him to make the heroic decision he did.

From Ross-shire he proceeded, in July of 1876, to Edinburgh, there to try his fortune. Here his early "goodness" melted away "as a morning cloud and the early dew." He attended meetings of the Christadelphians—a sect who deny the deity of Christ—and there learned his first lessons in atheism. He caused his companions intense concern by openly avowing himself an atheist, and sneering at things they had taught him to regard as sacred. Possessing a vigorous and inquiring mind he progressed rapidly in his new views, and among his companions affected a very supercilious and boastful air when religious questions were being discussed. Concurrent with his changed sentiments in regard to revelation a process of moral deterioration set in, happily, however, arrested ere he had pursued to any extent a life of folly. In this unsatisfactory state, after spending some time in Edinburgh, Macgregor proceeded to Newcastle-on-Tyne. The irregularity of habits begun in Edinburgh were for a time continued in Newcastle. Here, however, becoming alarmed, he became a total abstainer, and remained such to the end of life. He became a warm supporter of the Good Templar movement, and it was in connection with this work that his powers as a fluent and impressive speaker received their first development.

In applying for work at one of the Newcastle shops he met with an amusing rebuff. In the smaller towns of Scotland there is of necessity less sub-division of work in the various trades than obtains in the cities, where men are trained to the manufacture of a very limited class of articles. Thus, a joiner who is an expert at door-making, may know nothing of window-frame making. Macgregor had had experience in all branches of his trade, but he had yet to learn that it would not be advantageous to profess too much.

"What can you do?" asked the foreman.

"Anything, sir," was the ingenuous reply.

"You are far too clever for us!" was the sarcastic retort, and the applicant walked away.

Before applying at the next shop, Macgregor, with characteristic Scottish caution, took care to ascertain in what particular line trade was briskest, which he found to be door-making.

"What can you do?" was again the question.

"Make doors, sir," was the philosophic reply.

After being engaged at door-making for some time the work was nearly exhausted, when Macgregor suggested, with some trepidation, that he could also make window-frames. Whatever incredulity this gave rise to was removed when he was permitted to make the experiment.

While in Newcastle he had, what may be termed, a miraculous escape. He had been fitting window sashes at a height of about seventy feet from the ground. The slight scaffolding on which he was working suddenly gave way, and he fell a distance of between forty and fifty feet, on an awning covering sculptors who were at work underneath. The awning was crushed in, but it broke the fall, and enabled two of the sculptors to seize hold of him before being precipitated to the bottom. Though considerably bruised and shaken he was soon able to be at work again. During the erection of the same building several fellow-workmen were killed. What impression the circumstances made on Macgregor's mind at the time is not known; but, in after days, when brought to his "right mind," he felt profoundly thankful to God for His preserving care.

From Newcastle, early in 1878, he proceeded by steamer to London, there more fully to develop his sceptical opinions. He soon became a well-known exponent of materialistic views to the crowds of young men who throng the "Midland Arches," King's Cross.

His letters home reveal no diminished affection, but are in strong contrast with those he was so soon to pen. At this time home news and London sight-seeing filled up the entertaining pages; a little later, as we shall see, his letters, more copious and frequent, were toned with intense and affectionate solicitude for the spiritual well-being of the individual members of his family. The local news and the sights of London gave place to accounts of the work of God, in which he was heartily engaged.

One or two brief extracts may be given from his letters in 1878, as indicative of his state of mind at that time (though he seems studiously to have avoided reference to his sceptical opinions). Writing to his mother he says:—

" . . . A thousand thanks, dear mother, for your kind present. They fit me to a nicety. It was very kind of you to send them all this long way. I really wish I were in a position to do something for you—that I could express my feelings in acts, in fact. Do you know, mother, I often feel sad—grieved—when I think of you all at home. Of late I often have an irrepressible desire to be at home once more among you. I do not think, if spared, it will be long before I do come home. However, never mind that just now: it can't be for a little while yet. . . .

"I spent my holiday at the Alexandra Palace. My word, it is a glorious spot! Beautiful! I spent the whole day in the grounds. . . . And there is the Crystal Palace and grounds! Oh, such a grand building and lovely grounds! The job I am working on just now is within a stone-throw of Buckingham Palace."

Here is an extract from another letter. The tints are not so bright:—

"My dear Mother,—Please excuse me for not writing you before now. I would have done so, but that I was putting it off—as I am out of work for a few days—till I get a start. I have not got one yet, but I hope soon to have. It is not for the want of looking. I have been walking round the houses all day, but things are so dull—nothing doing in the trade. However, I am bound to have a job somewhere. . . .

"I was down at Woolwich, and saw the wreck and scene of the disaster, and brought home with me a bit of the paddle-box of the *Princess Alice*, just where the

Bywell Castle struck her. Oh, it has been an awful affair !"

The terrible catastrophe referred to, in which many hundreds of persons lost their lives, took place on Tuesday evening, September 3, 1878.

CHAPTER II.

CONVERSION.

VISIT HOME—CIRCULATES INFIDEL LITERATURE—SUDDEN CONVERSION AND OPEN CONFESSION—A YOUNG BROTHER'S SCEPTICISM—PROGRESS IN THE DIVINE LIFE—RETURN TO LONDON—THE YOUNG CONVERT'S FIRST LETTER.

ON the 31st of December, 1878, Macgregor surprised his friends at home by unexpectedly appearing among them. While they rejoiced to see him, they were shocked at the now unconcealed change in his religious views. He was scornful of all things sacred, and though he consented to attend Church on the succeeding Sabbath, he turned his attendance there into an occasion for jesting at the truth preached. He had gone further even than this. He brought with him from London a parcel of infidel literature, with the intention of disseminating sceptical views among his old companions, several of whom had come under the influence of divine grace. Boastful in his infidelity and eager to bring others under the baneful spell, he at once began the work on which his heart was set. But God had other purposes in view, and Macgregor was not many days at home when the Holy Spirit used means to dispel his scepticism, and to bring him, in genuine contrition, to the feet of Jesus. The means employed were not such as man would have thought adequate. The incident may itself seem trivial, "but God hath chosen the foolish things of the world to confound the wise; and God hath chosen the weak things of the world to confound the things which are mighty, . . . that no flesh should glory in His presence."

With his set purpose in view he attacked a former associate and school-fellow—Norman Ross, then recently converted, and studying at the time for mission work in China.

A remark made by Macgregor to Ross indicates his state of mind at this time, and also his ardent temperament. The remark has a significance, too, for professing Christians.

"Do you mean to tell me," he asked, "that if you really believed that all who pass up and down this street will be eternally lost if they do not trust in Jesus Christ, you could sit down so quietly, and show no more concern than Christians usually do? Why, if I could only believe what you profess to believe I would go out and stop the people in the street to tell them of their danger."

This was exactly what he did a little while after, and it became a daily habit. In the work-shop, on the street, and in the railway carriage, he sought opportunity to interest his fellow-men in the concerns of their souls' salvation. "Many a time," writes one, "have I seen him, with that sweet, happy smile of peace on his countenance, plead with some passer-by, whose attention he had previously secured by means of a tract."

But to resume the story. A long but friendly argument ensued between Macgregor and Ross, of which only the concluding part is known. They had been arguing on the point of whether man is wholly or only partially sinful. Ross who had been maintaining that "whosoever shall keep the whole law, and yet offend in one point, he is guilty of all," recalling the fact that Macgregor was an ardent advocate of Good Templary, said—

"Why, man, you are a Good Templar, but if you take a small sip of whisky what becomes of your pledge? Are you a Templar any longer?"

"I see it! I see it!" replied Macgregor, thoughtfully.

"Thank God," said Ross, surprised at the sudden change in his friend's manner; "but what do you see?"

"I see that I am a lost sinner, and that there *is* a God!"

The result was as gratifying to Ross, as it was surprising. There and then, after further conversation and prayer, Macgregor was led to accept the Lord Jesus Christ as his personal Saviour. How complete was his surrender to Christ, and how devoted his allegiance to His service, succeeding pages will tell. Between the two companions, so strangely brought together that day, a deep brother-like affection sprang up which lasted throughout life, and which, we cannot help thinking, has been perpetuated and deepened in the glory, into which both were in so short a time to enter.

Norman Ross's heart was full of China and its evangelisation, and it is touching to know that amid declining health and the straitened circumstances it induced, he bravely strove with his studies, if by any means he might be qualified for missionary work in that vast heathen country. It was Ross's passion in the matter, possibly, that gave the original bias to Macgregor's future course.

Macgregor made no secret of the radical change in his sentiments, and from the first took up a bold attitude in witnessing for Him whom he had so long and bitterly blasphemed. On parting with Ross, he at once told the good news to his astonished friends at home. They scarcely knew what to make of it. They were incredulous, but hopeful. The change in his conduct was undoubted, but the transformation was so sudden they dreaded it might prove ephemeral. Not so Macgregor himself. As soon as he found his feet in the narrow way, he became a swift runner in the course, and his pace never faltered. His career was brief, but in it there were no loiterings and no backslidings. That he had his share of imperfection cannot be doubted, but from the moment he put his hand to the plough he was never known to look back. His path from the first was stedfastly "Upward, onward, homeward, heavenward—looking unto Jesus."

After informing his parents of the change wrought in his soul by the Holy Spirit, he at once gathered together the infidel literature he had brought north, and consigned all to the flames—*not all*, however, for his youngest brother, Tom, a boy singularly precocious, and of a speculative mind, had appropriated some of the pamphlets. Tom's mind was at this time unfortunately only too susceptible to confirmation in sceptical ideas. These ideas were originally suggested to his own mind by what he considered the inconsistency of the average professing Christian, as compared with the ideal, and were strengthened by discussions with others who held more pronounced opinions. What Macgregor's self-reproachings must have been, may be imagined, when he discovered that his own young brother, for whom he entertained a peculiar affection, had, after his departure, been too surely confirmed in scepticism by the perusal of the books that escaped the fire. It needed much prayer to God and earnest personal remonstrance to undo the mischief. The answer to prayer was for a time delayed, but when granted, the younger Macgregor became as marked for his piety and zeal as his elder brother.

A few days after his conversion Macgregor called upon the late Rev. Dr. John Kennedy, the pastor of his boyhood, to whom he revealed the change that had taken place. Dr. Kennedy, after conference, commended him in prayer to the grace of God.

Macgregor's stay at home was prolonged for a week or two, during which he was an earnest student of his Bible. He was observed to be much in prayer during the remainder of his visit, and occupied his time mainly in taking long solitary walks in the neighbourhood. Though modest and retiring during that period, his trust in God was bright and pronounced. He was making very perceptible progress in the divine life, and to intimate friends he spoke of little else than his newly-found hope. Those who cared not for these things soon learned to shun his companionship. At home his affections deepened and mellowed, and his life there was characterised with abounding joy and self-forgetfulness. The leave-taking, on his return to London, was keenly felt both by his parents and himself.

The following letter, written to his mother immediately after his arrival in London, forms a contrast to the extracts with which the first chapter is concluded. We should mention that his friend Norman Ross had meanwhile also left Dingwall and returned to Edinburgh. The young convert writes :—

"21 Mabledon Place,
Euston Road, London, W.C.

"My dear Mother,—I trust this note may find you all in health. Thanks be to God our Father, who has brought us* to our journey's end in safety.

"When we got to Edinburgh Norman was at the station meeting us, and after ascertaining that we could break our journey, we resolved to stay all that day and night in Edinburgh. And, oh, I was so glad that I did stay, for we had a splendid time of it—*speaking about Jesus*—and not only about, but *with* Jesus. I could not tell you, although I should try, dear mother, how I enjoyed that short season, and how it strengthened me in the faith.

"Dear mother, tell father to be remembering me when he approaches the Throne of Grace.

"I saw D. M. in Edinburgh. He is a fine lad, and a real Christian. I also saw and had a talk with A. M.—

* A companion travelled with him.

he is a gem of a Christian. And poor dear Norman was so kind to me. Oh, I love Norman as a brother. He loves the Lord with all his heart, and one cannot help loving those who love *Him* who did so much for us.

"We left Edinburgh at half-past ten on Wednesday night, and got into London about half-past eight next morning. . . . We are just going to bed; we got scarcely any sleep since we left home, and are quite done up."

The letter concludes with affectionate remembrances to all his friends at home, and expressions of solicitude for a companion in whose spiritual well-being he was deeply interested.

CHAPTER III.

UPWARD AND ONWARD.

ENTHUSIASM IN CHRISTIAN WORK—A FELLOW-TOWNSMAN'S TESTIMONY—EARNEST REMONSTRANCES—HOW TO READ THE BIBLE—HOW SABBATH WAS SPENT—INDISPOSITION —SOLICITUDE FOR A SISTER'S SALVATION.

ARRIVED in London, Macgregor at once plunged into Christian work with all-consuming enthusiasm, so much so that his fellow-workmen, and companions, among whom, we have reason to believe, he was formerly a general favourite, could not understand the change. One of them, indeed, wrote to friends in the North, that Macgregor, in his earnestness, had "gone out of his mind!" It was the old story. The "world" can appreciate enthusiasm in every direction but one. "And when His friends heard of it," we read of Christ Himself, "they went out to lay hold on Him, for they said "He is beside Himself" (Mark iii. 21); others said "He hath a devil and is mad" (John x. 20). "Paul thou art beside thyself," exclaimed Festus, "much learning doth make thee mad" (Acts xxvi. 24).

" We are fools for Christ's sake," is Paul's own admission (1 Cor. iv. 10); and his defence is—" For whether we be beside ourselves, it is to God; or whether we be sober, it is for your cause" (2 Cor. v. 13.) A few weeks previously Macgregor had left London a boastful sceptic, he returned subdued and changed, and with his zeal running in new channels. The change was marvellous. " They went out to see what was done; . . . and found the man, out of whom the devils were departed, clothed, and in his right mind; and they were afraid" (Luke viii. 35).

The thoroughness of the change is thus testified to by a fellow-townsman :—

" Our beloved departed brother, Mr. Wm. M. Macgregor, and I were brought up in the same Scottish burgh, and attended the same class in the Sabbath School. At that time neither of us knew the Lord. When I next met him it was in London. I had been converted about four years previously, and having ascertained his address, I went to speak to him of the things concerning his soul's welfare. In our conversation, if he mentioned God, he would add, 'If there be a God.'

" One thing struck me much. He said 'If I believed that there was a hell I would go and tell every person I met of his danger.' I took out my Testament, and he took out his 'Tom Paine.' After a little time I left him, and thought his was about the hardest case I had ever met with.

" A few months subsequently I was surprised by his calling on me. He said he came to apologise for the manner in which he had treated me on the occasion of my visiting him. With great joy he told me of his conversion, and of the surpassing love of Christ. We then fell on our knees, and he poured out his heart unto God with such fervour, thankfulness, praise, and humility, that I almost felt awed in his presence. I had known Jesus long before he had, but I was humbled, and ashamed that I knew so little, in comparison with him, of the sweetness and gladness of the love and presence of Jesus. He had found not only salvation, but also the abiding presence of the Lord Jesus to comfort and sustain him at all times."

On the first Sabbath in London after his conversion he visited the "Midland Arches," King's Cross, where he had so frequently joined with others in denying and blaspheming God, and there publicly declared that his views had been completely changed, that he was now converted to God, and boldly avowed his allegiance to the Lord Jesus Christ and His cause.

He joined the Goldington Crescent Presbyterian Church, of which he afterwards became one of the "managers," and under the stimulating pastorate of the Rev. Mr Woffendale, whose self-denying labours and open-air preachings in and around King's Cross are well known in the district, he threw himself with great enthusiasm into all the aggressive work carried on in connection with Mr. Woffendale's congregation. Every Sabbath afternoon he was to be seen telling forth the merits of the Saviour he had so recently learned to love to the thousands who gathered round the Bandstand in Regent Park. From Regent Park it was his custom to proceed, at a later hour, to engage in similar work at the Cobden Statue, Camden Town. In the winter months, when open-air preaching was impossible, Mr. Woffendale rented, for religious services during week-day evenings, King's Cross Theatre, where Macgregor, under the leadership of his pastor, and in company with a band of like-spirited Christian workers, found congenial employment. Earnestly engaged in this and other work of a like nature, and with many tokens of God's favour, the months passed happily by.

A few extracts from his letters will indicate his rising spiritual temperature. Writing to his mother, he says:—

"Mother, when we come to our death-bed, when we feel the coldness of death coming over us, when, perchance, our friends who may be standing around us are weeping, and we can scarcely see them, and their voices are sounding as far away, and we are slipping away into eternity—oh, mother, if in that hour we are going, we know not where—if our weary souls are not resting on Christ—then, oh, what a fearful state to stand in before the bar of God. . . . God says, 'To-day, if you will hear my voice, harden not your hearts'; 'Now is the accepted time, now is the day of salvation.'"

To his youngest brother he writes, on April 8th, 1879, after speaking of the unsatisfactory state of trade, and the long distance he had to walk to and from his work:—

"It is, however, good to have something to do; and,

my dear brother, it is a grand and glorious thing to know we have God as our Father, and Jesus as our Friend and Elder Brother. . . . Trusting everything to Jesus we are in a position to feel, and to understand, and to be comforted by the many, many promises in the blessed Word, that God will never leave us nor forsake us. . . . Just read the 37th Psalm (prose). . . . Tom, my dear brother, *be seeking Jesus*. . . . Give my love to David [the now only surviving member of the family, besides his mother]; tell him to read the 5th and 6th chapters of Romans, and study what Paul says. Love to my father and my mother, and also to Annie and Johannie. I have a lot to tell you, but must be done to-night. Good night, boys! May God bless you all. I am praying to my Father for you all every time I think of you."

Ten days later he writes to his brothers, intimating that his health was not good, and that he was out of work—

"But 'the Lord is my Shepherd; I shall not want!' Thank God for His loving-kindness to us in times gone by. And we know that whosoever puts his trust in the Lord Jesus Christ alone will never want any good thing. (Psalm xxxiv. 9, 10; and again Phil. iv. 19.) Praise God for His mercy. . . . Why I write to-day is because I noticed the paper (enclosed) in the window of the office of the *Fountain*, and thought one of you two boys—or both of you—might try to win the prize. Even though you do not succeed the searching of the Scriptures would do you good. If you do try I will give you one advice: every time you open your

Bibles to look for anything, go down on your knees, and lift up your hearts to God in prayer that He may do for you what Jesus did for the two men with whom He walked to Emmaus—that he may open the Scriptures to you. . . . My dear brothers, trust in Jesus. Do not make any preparation, but just say 'Lord Jesus, save me, or I perish!'"

The advice here given, to kneel down and ask God's blessing before reading the Bible, was the regular practice of Macgregor himself, and may have accounted for his deep spirituality. In learning the Chinese language, this trait much impressed his native teacher.

A month later (in May) he writes that he has found employment, but that its continuance is uncertain. The undercurrent of sadness is pardonable. Discipline was doing its salutary work—

"R. J. is still with me. Oh, he has lots of kind friends—cousins and many other relatives—to whose houses he is constantly going either to dinner or tea. Mr —— and Mr —— are among his backers. But, my dear brother, we have *One* to *back* us, with whom such as these are not worthy to be compared—even *Jesus*. We have the Father, Son, and Holy Spirit. Are we not truly blessed? I am always praying to our Father that He may so bless you that you may be enabled to find that true peace and joy which pass all understanding. And, oh, Davie, be sure to ask our blessed Lord to save every one of our sisters and brothers, and all who are near and dear to us. Then what a glorious future to look forward to—when our work on earth is done, that we should all meet together, and be with Jesus for ever in that heavenly Home, where there will be no more sorrow or trial. . . . May God grant that we shall all meet in the Celestial City,

> "'In the bright beyond the river
> Where the surges cease to flow.'

"I may tell you how I employ my time on the Sabbath. Well, I go first, at 10 A.M., to the Young Men's Fellowship meeting, in Regent Square; at 11 A.M. to Church, till 1 P.M.; then at a quarter from 3 till 4 I teach a class in the Sunday School; next I attend a teachers' meeting; then go to Church again, and generally end with an open-air service, of which I shall tell you more again."

The foregoing will give an idea of Macgregor's state of mind during the summer months of 1879. His health was not quite satisfactory during this period, and caused himself and his friends some anxiety. In December he writes—

"I have not gone to a physician as yet, but I intend to do so as soon as I can. I have a bad cough, and have had it, I may say, ever since I came back to London. . . . Oh, dear mother, let us take all our griefs to Jesus, our dearest Friend, who is ever ready to hear and to help us."

On December 15, 1879, Macgregor wrote to one of his brothers as follows. A comparison of the extract with his letters of six months previous will show that he was growing spiritually :—

"I hope you will forgive me [for delay in writing] when you know that I am about my Father's business. I hope you are growing in grace, my dear brother. Oh, Davie, keep close to Jesus. Be constantly praying to God. Prayer will make the devil give way. Prayer, Davie, is the bell-rope reaching from earth to heaven, and, if by faith you lay hold on this rope, you can ring the bell in heaven. Oh, my brother, think of the glorious privilege we have of communing with, and receiving a welcome and blessing from, the mighty and everlasting God. . . . Oh, thank God that Jesus shed His precious blood that guilty sinners such as we might have life. 'Thanks be to God for His unspeakable Gift!' . . . I send you one of my *cartes*. . . . I look a little happier than in the *carte* last taken. Now, may the grace of the Lord Jesus Christ, and the blessing of God the Father, and the sweet communion and fellowship of the Holy Spirit rest upon and abide with each and every one of you all evermore. Amen, and amen."

In January of 1880 he was still anxious about his health, and had obtained medical advice. The symptoms, he believed, were alarming, and for several days he thought his life was in the balance. While still in ill-health, and out of work, he did not forget his friends. His heart broods over their spiritual well-being. He wrote to his younger sister on February 10th, 1880, that his health, though unsatisfactory, was improving. He begins the letter (as became his almost invariable custom afterwards) by prefacing it with a verse of Scripture :—

"Seek ye the Lord, while He may be found; call ye upon Him while He is near."

"My dearest sister, Jo,—. . . I am praying for you, that God's Holy Spirit may work in your heart, and make you feel your need of a Saviour. Oh, Jo, I will never be truly happy until every one of my brothers and sisters are safe in the fold of the Good Shepherd. My dear sister, while you are young give your heart to Jesus. He is willing, and able, and anxious, to save you; . . . and instead of your old and wicked heart, He will give you a new and clean heart—a heart of obedience to Himself. That God may help and bless you, Jo, is the prayer of your affectionate brother,

"WILLIE.

"P.S.—I wish I could say 'your brother in Jesus.' Write me soon, and tell me what you are thinking about your soul."

CHAPTER IV.

THOUGHTS OF BECOMING A MISSIONARY, AND ABOUNDING LABOURS.

OPEN-AIR PREACHING—WORK IN COMMON LODGING-HOUSES—TESTIFYING FOR JESUS ON PENTONVILLE ROAD—FIRST THOUGHTS OF BECOMING A MISSIONARY—DEATH OF A CHRISTIAN BROTHER—ELDEST SISTER'S CONVERSION—STRONG NATURAL FEELINGS—HOW HE SPENT HIS TIME—FLIGHT OF TIME, AND REALITY OF ETERNITY—CHANGED VIEWS ON BAPTISM--PLEADING WITH HIS YOUNGER BROTHER—SOLICITUDE FOR NORMAN ROSS.

AS 1880 sped on its way, it found Macgregor "in labours more abundant." The work of soul-saving with him became a passion. His interest in the thousands of young men who, careless and indifferent as to their eternal welfare, thronged the streets on Sabbath, was very great. He felt that the most likely means of reaching them was by declaring in manly tones the simple narrative of the plan of salvation at the corners of busy thoroughfares. Whilst walking along Pentonville Road one evening with a friend to whom he was much attached—Dr. Parry, now of the China Inland Mission, but then a medical student in the London Hospital—he suddenly said—

"What a splendid spot for an open-air meeting! What do you say if we just testify for Jesus here?"

Mr Parry cordially assented, and so, without further preliminaries, the two young men, in felt weakness, but in humble dependence upon God's help, took up their stand at the corner of Claremont Square and Pentonville Road. Taking off their hats, they asked God to send them those whose hearts He had prepared to receive the truth, and at the conclusion of the prayer a goodly number of people had gathered, to whom they declared the gospel message. At the close of the meeting several persons came forward to shake them warmly by the hand, and to thank them for their words of life and hope; and at the request of several Christians they agreed to hold a similar service there every Sabbath evening. Thus was begun a work for God which He has blessed to the salvation of many souls. Afterwards they held the meeting on the other side of the Pentonville Road, opposite a large public-house, and adjoining the North London Secular Society's Hall, by the members of which much hostility was shown.

"I shall never forget," says his brother, who furnishes the above particulars, "coming to this meeting with my dear brother, the first Sabbath evening after my arrival in London, in August, 1881. This was the first time I had seen him since he had left home after his conversion, and the change in him was wonderful. I felt the truth and force of a remark made by one who was led into the liberty of the truth by his preaching, "Ah, the glory of Heaven shines in that young man's face!"

Macgregor's success as an evangelist was undoubted. Mr Broomhall, secretary of the China Inland Mission, records of him and a little band of companions, that it was their practice, on Saturdays, to attend, first, a missionary prayer meeting, have tea, afterwards hold a prayer meeting among themselves, "and then sally forth for open-air preaching in Hoxton. Again and again have they had to rejoice over striking cases of clear and decided conversion to God in connection with these services, and over many backsliders reclaimed. In this work Macgregor was pre-eminently useful, none being listened to with more attention or by a larger number of people."

The same incidents, with a few added particulars, are referred to in the Report for 1880 of the Islington and Highbury Branch of the Young Men's Christian Association:—

"In May we took our stand, four young workers, by the New River reservoir. Shortly some helpers joined us in singing, and we rejoiced to see so many staying to listen. The services were continued till the beginning of October. The audiences became larger, and though near a secular hall, the quiet and attention manifested were remarkable. No prolonged and fruitless arguments disturbed us, for which we were grateful; we refrained not from speaking to the best of our ability upon unbelief from the moral and spiritual side. And the thrilling testimony of one brother, who was himself saved from infidelity, has often been most eagerly listened to by the people; and as we watched the faces of the listeners, we could see that there was a real work of grace going on. . . .

"After the brother above mentioned had finished his earnest pleadings for the people to receive the Saviour at once many hands were held out to grasp his, and many a 'God bless you' has come from old and young. One little token in a nice, kind letter was given from one who had found that the services had been a great blessing."

Next year the entire charge of this work, and also the superintendentship of the "Lodging-House Mission" was undertaken by Macgregor. These "Common Lodging-Houses" are the temporary abodes of men and women who by misfortune or misconduct have fallen low in the social scale. In these houses—some of which are capable of accommodating several hundreds of persons—a night's shelter can be obtained for payment of sums varying from threepence to one shilling. The payment entitles each lodger to the use of a large fire and the simplest of utensils, with which to cook his food. It was Macgregor's practice, with two or three companions, to visit three of these houses every Sunday evening and read and expound a portion of Scripture. The work was of an exceedingly difficult and trying character, but it is believed the efforts were not without blessing in many cases.

To his younger brother he wrote, on June 15, as follows. This letter contains one of the earliest hints of his desire to be a missionary—

"My dear Brother,—I do wish we were all here together. I know it would be better, for a hundred reasons. It would be better for *me.* Everything *goes* here—clothes and money—and as for comfort and anything like home, these are not to be thought of. However, *the Lord is with me.* Glory be to Jesus. Oh, it is an awfully real world to some—this London. You have not the least conception of what real life in London is. Oh, the wickedness; oh, the shams; oh the hollowness of everything! I tell you, dear brother, I just write on it all, 'Vanity of vanities, all is vanity.' Really I would not remain here as I am one week longer if it were not for the one aim of my life now.

"And, my dear brother, although you may not altogether agree with me in cherishing the thought of my going abroad, I do believe God intends sending me out as a missionary some day. However grieved I might be, or however much wounded your hearts might be for a season, still I am willing to go, and to lay down my life, if need be, for my dear Lord and Master's sake. I just mention this to you that you may know what keeps me in London. Do not mention anything of this to anybody, as I know nothing definitely yet.

"Love to all the dear ones at home, from one who loves you all dearly. I commit you all to the care of Him who neither slumbers nor sleeps.

"WILLIE."

This letter is cross-written, and the blank spaces are filled up with Scripture texts appealing to his brother to decide for Christ—a practice which he continued in all his letters home.

On the 6th of August 1880, the death occurred in Dingwall, of an earnest and consistent Christian young man, whose example and counsel had been very helpful to young Christians, who loved to gather round his sick-bed. The event caused Macgregor to write—

"So our brother, John Macdonald, has *gone in to see the King!* 'Blessed are the dead which die in the Lord.' Many, I am sure, will miss our brother. That is one less in the vineyard, which means more love, more zeal, in those who are left behind. Oh, that the Lord Himself would stir up the cold, dead, half-hearted Christians, who are at ease in Zion. Oh, that the lips of every true servant of God were touched with a live coal from off the altar. I do wish that the glad good news of salvation through the blood of the Lamb were carried from house to house and from shop to shop, till at the name of JESUS every knee shall bow and every tongue confess. Oh, may God help us to be faithful unto death that so we may win the crown. . . .

"From your affectionate boy

"WILLIE.

"P.S.—'We have redemption through His blood, even the forgiveness of sins'! (Col. i. 14).

"'He that believeth HATH everlasting life.'"

A work of grace had at this time been in progress in Dingwall among the young men in connection with the Y.M.C.A. It was a testing time for the young converts. Macgregor, after referring to the matter in a letter to his eldest brother, says :—

"Cling to Jesus, in spite of all disappointments or crosses. Pray, pray—pray continually at your work, or wherever you may be. Be always communing with God. And do not for a moment allow hard thoughts about any one to lodge in your heart. Pray the Lord our Saviour Jesus to take all uncharitable thoughts out of your mind. We are so apt to think hard thoughts of others who do not seem to us to do as they ought to do.

"'Ask the Saviour to help you,
Comfort, and strengthen, and keep you,
He is willing to aid you ;
He will carry you through.'"

Macgregor's eldest sister—Annie—had about this period been converted to God, and the event caused him much joy. She was desirous to proceed to London, but this proposal did not meet with her brother's approval, and he wrote :—

"God sent you there for a glorious purpose. Do you not see the hand of God in it? He *sent you away from home* to get converted, and He *brought me home* to get converted. Truly the Lord works in mysterious ways! . . .

"Well now, Annie, I really do not know what to say, or how to advise you. In the first place, I am very unsettled myself. I am far from being as I would like to be. In fact, I do not think I would stay twenty minutes in London were it not for just this—God has saved me ; I belong to Jesus, body, soul, and spirit ;

and He has a right to do with me just as He pleases. Now I have it firmly fixed in my mind that He wants me to go and bear a message from Himself to the poor heathen, who bow down to wood and stone—I believe God wants me to be a missionary. In order to this I believe He has laid it on my heart to try to get into a College, or Training Institute, for students of His Word. I can scarcely think of anything else night or day. . . .

"Meanwhile I am lifting up my voice inside and outside, in street corners and *everywhere* He leads me, proclaiming the glad tidings of great joy—God's wondrous love to guilty and hell-deserving sinners, and, God helping me, dear Annie, I mean to continue to tell out the old, old story of Jesus and His love. I glory in the Cross of our Lord Jesus Christ, and while God gives me strength to stand, and breath to speak, I will

"'Tell of His mighty love,
Mighty to save.'

"Oh, Annie, pray for me, and ask father and every one of the family to remember me, as I remember you, in prayer. Ask the Lord to make me faithful, and to make all crooked ways straight for me, and to make and keep me humble and low down at His dear feet. . . .

"Annie dear, follow Jesus. Don't be ashamed of Jesus, but glory in our dear Redeemer."

This letter does more than breathe the spirit of consecration—it indicates some of the conditions necessary in a life of consecration. The mind was in him, in no small degree, which was also in Christ Jesus, whom he loved so well: "The zeal of thine house hath eaten me

D

up;" "Wist ye not that I must be about my Father's business?" Zeal for God's cause, however, did not wither up natural feeling. Rather it mellowed it, and also deepened it.

"I ought to feel thankful to God," he writes to his mother, "that I have a father and a mother, whose hearts yearn after their boy; and, dear mother, God only knows how often I think over you at home, and how often the remembrances of home, with all its comforts, and its cheerfulness, and its peace, and all that goes to make up a happy home, make me shed tears. I often wish I could recall those happy days long gone by—never to return—when as little children we romped about together, and went to the old school. I might ask, Where are they all now—those once happy children? Ah, some are scattered the world over, in every clime; the bodies of some lie in foreign lands; some sleep in the ocean's depths, and we trust their souls have gone to that *better land*. . . . Ah, dear mother, when I look back a few years only how many instances of God's love and sparing mercy can I recall. How often has He preserved me in the midst of dangers you do not know anything about. Oh, what ought I to do for God for all His preserving mercies—He preserved me in the midst of dangers when I was a careless, open scoffer at His Holy Word—a sinner hell-deserving. But thanks be to God I can now say with David—'He brought me up also out of an horrible pit, out of the miry clay, and set my feet upon a Rock, and established my goings, and He put a new song in my mouth, even praise unto *our* God.' . . .

"Well, mother, the fact is, I give every moment I can spare to the service of Him who hath redeemed me. I will give you an idea of how I spend my time. As the Lord hath given me a talent for speaking, I am always engaged in trying to set before perishing souls the glorious plan of salvation. My whole soul is in it, and I wish you would at home pray for me that the Lord might bless me in all things. . . .

"May God grant that we all may meet in heaven—a family united in Christ. It is such a simple thing—it is gloriously simple, and simply glorious!—just to come to Jesus as sinners, nothing else—nothing but as hell-deserving sinners—and His promise is that 'whosoever cometh unto Me, I will in no wise cast out.'"

A programme of the week's work in connection with Goldington Crescent Presbyterian Church, Pancras Road, is inclosed in the letter. It shows work for every night of the week—meetings for prayer, praise, giving in reports, &c.; open-air services in various parts of London; temperance meetings; Sabbath schools, &c. Macgregor adds—

"All of those meetings I regularly attend, and have to speak at the Monday, Tuesday, Thursday, Saturday, and Sunday meetings. Oh, it is glorious, working for Jesus; and, remember, all this working is not to obtain salvation. Oh, no, for then we would be fools. It is simply because we love Jesus and He has redeemed us and washed us in His precious blood, that we want others to come and receive the free gift from God, which is eternal life through our Lord Jesus Christ."

It will be seen that no value was set on these abounding labours as a ground of merit. It was his love to do the will of God, and his desire that others should receive the blessing he so highly esteemed, that nerved him onwards. He was also impressed with the brevity of time, and the endurance of eternity. He says—

"I would write oftener, but what with my daily work, and one thing and another, I am never a moment off my feet, except when getting a little sleep. London is such a world in itself, and one living in it has so many calls—here, there, and everywhere. You want to be in more places than one at a time—to attend this class and to go to that meeting. Oh, thank God for such blessed privileges. I love to be with God's children. I love to hear the name of Jesus, my glorious Redeemer, who gave Himself for me. . . . The days, and weeks, and years are flying—speeding along into eternity! Oh, the reality of eternity! All here is but shadow. You grasp it, and it is gone. There is nothing real but God and eternity. . . . Oh, God, may none of us be at ease in Zion; may God keep us from having the lamp of profession, without the oil of the Spirit!"

During 1880 Macgregor's views on the question of baptism underwent a change, with the result that he was re-baptized, and, leaving the Presbyterian Church, joined the Baptists. The wrench was keenly felt, for it involved dissociation from a large body of earnest active Christian workers, in whose loving fellowship he found great spiritual joy and help. In his letters home he spoke little of his changed sentiments.

His labours in London continued incessant and fruitful, and his letters to friends became increasingly fervent. Meanwhile his friend, Norman Ross, fell into decline, and had in consequence to return from Edinburgh to Dingwall. Macgregor writes home—

"Dear brother, give me all the news of Dingwall; and, Tom, privately, just tell me all you know of the state of Norman Ross's health. Is he consumptive? or is it just a severe cold? or what is the matter with poor Norman? Poor, dear fellow, remember me kindly to him, and tell him I am to write him shortly. And now, dear Tom, just allow me to say a word or two to you, my own dear brother, about your soul. Is the great question settled with you yet? You are now growing up, and this is a matter we have each to decide for himself. We have to deal with God individually, and you know the Lord Jesus said, 'Ye must be born again,' or 'from above.' . . . If you look at the 3rd chapter of Romans, 22nd and 23rd verses, you will see that God says, 'There is no difference.' There is a difference in degree, but not of guilt. 'All have sinned, and come short.' But, oh, dear brother, what amazing love is that of God to us. Just think of God speaking and pleading with us to come and be reconciled, as He is satisfied with the death of Christ in our place. Read Rom. v. 8-11; also Eph. ii. 1-10. Oh, dear brother, if you have not as yet given your heart to Jesus do it now. Just tell Him all your mind, and trust Him for a full salvation. 'He that believeth on the Son *hath* everlasting life' (John iii. 36). May God Himself help you to put your whole trust in Jesus, for His name's sake. Amen."

It was thus he pled in many letters with his much-loved brother, whose young mind had been poisoned by infidelity. We shall see afterwards how God answered prayer, and blessed these tender appeals, not only in the case of Tom, but other members of the family. The reply to his inquiry regarding Norman Ross was not satisfactory, and he writes—

"I was so sorry to hear that poor dear Norman is so unwell. Poor fellow: and yet, Davie, he is an heir of God, a joint-heir with Christ (Rom. viii. 17). Pray for poor dear Norman that whatever our Father, in His infinite wisdom sees best to do with our dear brother, he may have grace given him to say, 'Thy will be done—not mine!' I do hope that God may be graciously pleased to send our beloved brother to carry the glad tidings to poor far-distant China. Oh, I should be so pleased; but our loving Father knows best."

CHAPTER V.

DECISION TO BECOME A MISSIONARY.

DEFINITE DECISION TO BE A MISSIONARY—THE CLAIMS OF CHINA—AN ENTIRE NIGHT OF PRAYER—NOT INCREASED IN WORLDLY GOODS—PLEADING WITH YOUNGEST BROTHER—DECLINING INTEREST IN ORDINARY NEWS—A DAY IN THE COUNTRY—BITTER MEMORIES—ONE SUBJECT OCCUPYING HIS THOUGHTS—TESTIMONY IN VIEW OF DEATH.

MACGREGOR'S letters for several months make no reference to his desire to become a missionary. The matter was not, however, absent from his thoughts, and on November, 16, 1880, he writes to his mother—

"Well now, my dear mother, after very long and prayerful consideration, and seeking of guidance from God, I have felt constrained to apply to a Foreign Missionary Society, as a candidate. I wish to go as a missionary to China. I have not done this rashly, as I have had a very serious impression for a long time that God wanted me to be a missionary. I did not, however, fully understand my own mind on the subject, and I kept praying about it, and in a very mysterious way God led me to a place where a prayer-meeting for China is held every week. This place I have attended for nearly a year, and now the great need of China is laid on my heart, and if God is willing to send me, I am quite willing to go and preach the glad tidings of great joy to the poor perishing millions in far-distant China. Will you all unite in praying for me that God's will may be done in regard to this matter. I have thought of the dangers, of the many trials, and of the possibility of my never returning to this dear land again; but, oh, dear mother, I hope I can say with Paul, 'None of these things move me.' If God will only accept of me I am willing to go, and, my own dear mother, I am sure you would be willing to give me up to Jesus for His work. And, dear father, too, would give up his son that he might go and be an ambassador for Christ. Oh, dear mother, God did not spare His own well-beloved Son, but freely gave Him up for us—for *you* and for *me*, and also just as much for the poor, dark, idolatrous Chinese. The Lord Jesus poured out His soul unto death to save us, and what is all we can do for Jesus compared with what He has done for us? Then just think of this. There are 400,000,000 of souls in China. One million die every month, or over 33,000 every twenty-four hours—all, or nearly all, perishing without having heard the name of Jesus! Does it not make your heart ache? And do you wonder that I feel constrained to offer myself as a missionary to these poor perishing millions? But while I am offering myself to the CHINA INLAND MISSION, I do not know whether I will be accepted or not, and in any case I shall likely have to wait for nearly a year—or perhaps more. So you see it is all in God's hands. I can do nothing but wait, and I know if God wants me to go I will go, and if not I will not. Will you all pray to God to make the way plain to me, that I may assuredly know what His will is?"

There is no reticence in speaking of China after this—

"I wish," he asks, "you would remember me always in your prayers, that God would guide me, and do with me just as He wills. If it is God's will to send me to China ask that my way may be opened up, and that all obstructions may be removed; and if it is not God's will pray that I may not go. I do not want to go unless I am sent out by my God; but if He sends me I am willing to go anywhere with Jesus."

In the letter to his mother he says he did not choose "rashly" to become a missionary. A fellow-townsman, from whose letter a quotation has already been made, states that they were together at a public meeting in Kilburn Hall, when the needs of China were laid before the Lord's people. On leaving this meeting Macgregor spoke of the impression made upon him, but was cautioned by his friend to make it quite certain the call was from God. The meeting was held on Easter Monday, 1881, and the speaker on China was Mr Maccarthy, of the China Inland Mission. "Some months later," wrote Mr Broomhall, in an "In Memoriam" notice in *China's Millions*, for February, 1883, "Macgregor accepted an invitation to a prayer-meeting held every Saturday afternoon at No. 2 Pyrland Road. To his surprise, he found that the meeting was for prayer for China. His impressions concerning his call to China were deepened; he came again and again to the meetings, and at length offered himself for the work."

Before his decision to become a missionary was fully formed, he spent an entire night with God on the subject. To use his own words—

"While I was bowed down in prayer before God about four o'clock in the morning, He suddenly filled my heart with the calm and settled conviction that He had accepted me for work in China, and from that hour I had not the least doubt but that, in His time and way, I should be sent out."

He at once intimated his desire to the China Inland Mission, and received with unbounded joy a short time afterwards, an invitation from Mr Broomhall, the Secretary of the Mission, to come and stay for a week or two at the "House." He interpreted this invitation as a clear indication that his way was to be opened up.

The year was closing; but in worldly affairs Macgregor had not much increased. His only regret, however, was that he was unable to help his friends at home. He says:—

"I do wish I were able to prove my affection for you all in a more substantial way than by words; but I am not, and I cannot help it. I am sure I try to do my best; and, thank God, He is kind to me. If I cannot command money, bless His holy name I can have peace and joy in the Lord, and have the love of Jesus shed abroad in my heart. . . . May God bless you all, and may you have a very happy (I do not say 'merry') Christmas; and, oh, let us, for Jesus' sake, begin the new year with a determination that whatsoever others may do, as for us and all our house *we* will serve the Lord."

To his brother Tom he wrote, on January 7, 1881, an affectionate letter, urging him to decide for Christ—

"There is but one thing needful to make 1881 a happy year, let the circumstances we are placed in be what they may—and that is the love of Christ in the heart. . . . Take this from me at the beginning of the year—

"'REMEMBER'.	Eccl. xii. 1.
"'SEEK' . .	Isa. lv. 6.
"'COME' . .	Isa. i. 18; John vii. 37; Matt. xi. 28.
"'BELIEVE' .	Acts xvi. 3; John v. 24; 1st John iii. 23.
"'TRUST' . .	2 Cor. i. 9: Psalms xxxiv. 8; xl. 4.

"Oh, my dearest brother, if you do this then you will be able to *love, obey, serve,* and *follow;* in which you will find PEACE, passing all understanding; JOY, unspeakable. . . .

"Oh, you are all so kind to me. My Heavenly Father has promised to supply the needs of all His own children, and, bless His holy name, He is faithful and unchangeable who has promised. Is it not glorious to be able to say in reality that 'The Lord is *my* Shepherd, *therefore* I shall not want?' . . . Dear brother, CHRIST IS THE GOOD SHEPHERD. Do you think He will ever let any of His sheep starve? Oh, no, never, never. I do thank God for the day I was led to trust Jesus. Do not be afraid to cast yourself upon Him. He *will* receive you."

The blank space over the date in this letter is filled in with these texts :—

"When a few years are come I shall go the way whence I shall not return" (Job xvi. 22); "We spend our years as a tale that is told" (Ps. xc. 9).

In a subsequent letter, he writes :—

"Now, dear brother, do not let me close without asking you once again if you have yet given your heart to the Lord Jesus Christ? if you have determined to renounce the world and its ways? and the devil and all his works? and be a disciple of the Lord Jesus? Beloved brother, do answer this question, if not to me, at least to God. Oh, Tom, do seek the Lord with all your heart and soul, and ask Him to give you His Holy Spirit to quicken your soul, and enlighten your mind, that you may feel your need of a Saviour, and also to bring you to Jesus, who is just the Saviour you and I need."

It must not be thought that, though religious subjects occupied so prominent a place in Macgregor's letters, they excluded everything else. His concern in all the interests of the family was real, but, beyond what affected them, secular affairs possessed a decreasing attraction. Now and again there is a passing allusion to other matters, but this is less frequent as his mind becomes absorbed in the one object for which he lived. He writes—

"Tom says I ought to have plenty of news in London. Well, yes, but really if you only knew how little interest I take in the things passing on around me you would not be surprised at my not giving you a budget of news when I write."

"Thanks for the *Ross-shire Journal*," he writes on July 15, 1881, "I am always glad to see it for the local news it contains. I was delighted to see that Tom's name was mentioned with such honour. It was a surprise to me, and I had a good cry over it. I felt so pleased that he is so persevering in his studies. . . . I also do not cease night and day to pray that he may be made a partaker of *the* wisdom of which the Apostle Paul speaks in 1 Cor. ii. 7."

The following shows that he was keenly susceptible to forms of recreation in which every healthy mind finds enjoyment. He writes on April 19th, 1881 :—

"I had a day in the country last Friday. Being Good Friday it was of course a general holiday (as well as Easter Monday), and in company with other three young Christians, I went for a day's walking in the country. We spent a glorious day. We took the train (or rather it took us !) to a station a few miles out of London. We then set off and tramped all round to Richmond and Kew, and other places. Oh, the country was beautiful ! It was my first day in the green fields since last summer, with the exception of a week at Hastings at

Christmas. No one who has not lived in London can understand what delight is to be found in getting out into the open country and into the pure fresh air again. We did enjoy ourselves! We lay down in Richmond Park, and read from God's two books—nature and Revelation. We sang praises to God, while around us the birds and all nature seemed to join in the song. We then went into a quiet little country churchyard, and had a small prayer meeting, lifting up our hearts to God. We afterwards started for hcme, doing a little for the Master by the way. Oh, I should so enjoy a few days during the summer up in the dear old country. I hope I may be able to have them if it is my Father's will.

"I am sure, dear mother, you sometimes think I might give you more news than I do when I write. Well, yes; I might fill sheets of paper with news of various kinds, but really I cannot take the trouble. I do not mean that it would be a trouble for me to write to you, but I do not trouble myself very much with the things that are taking place around me. Time is short, and the work is great, and we who are the Lord's own blood-bought servants must not, dare not, stand idle in the market place. No, no! We must be up and doing while it is day, for the night cometh when man cannot work. So, dear mother, my time is fully occupied.

"I hear that you are having a great awakening in the Highlands. Oh, I do pray that God may send forth His Holy Spirit with power into the hearts of all His true disciples in Dingwall. Oh, for a shaking of the dry bones; oh, for a mighty revival of true religion! May God grant it for Jesus' sake. . . . .

"You will see by the paper I send you that Lord Beaconsfield is dead."

Page after page is devoted to spiritual matters, and an historic event that interested the civilized world is dismissed with a mere reference. The leaven of the Kingdom of Heaven had surely well-nigh leavened the three measures of meal (Matt. xiii. 33).

Macgregor often referred to the time when he was a sceptic. The remembrance of it never failed to prompt feelings of profound gratitude to God, who raised him out of the horrible pit and from the miry clay. Writing on May 17th, 1881, of his brother, who was then leaving home he says:—

"And, oh, I do pray that he may never travel the road on which his brother went so far, but from which, thanks be to our merciful and gracious God, he has been rescued. To His name be glory for ever."

On August 1, he wrote:—

"My dearest Mother,— . . . I never hear a word from Dingwall—I may almost say Scotland—except from David and yourself, and one feels almost as if home were a beautiful dream, a dim recollection of something that is past. . . .

"I know that when I write I do not give you any news, or tell you of what I see and hear. But really, my dear mother, I cannot help it. You may think that I am always speaking about religion, and about our blessed Lord Jesus Christ. Well, I cannot help that either. If you knew how I think of you all at home, and pray that God may give to each of you whom I love the unspeakable blessing of salvation through His dear Son, and when I remember how dead everything around you is—having a name to live but yet dead—oh, I feel I must speak and determine to know nothing but Christ! How long we may be here none of us knows, and any one of us may be called away at a moment's notice. If so—if it were to-night—where would we be to-morrow? Surely nothing else ought to engage our attention till this all-important question is settled—blessedly settled—by our receiving from God that peace which alone can come from a knowledge of sins forgiven, and acceptance in the Beloved. May God the Holy Spirit convince of sin, enlighten the mind in the knowledge of the truth, by leading all to see in Christ Jesus the Lamb of God which taketh away the sin of the world. . . . The fact is, my dearest mother, one thing occupies my thoughts, by day and by night, and I can think of nothing else. Will you try and bear with me, and forgive me, when I seem to be careless, indifferent, or unsympathetic."

In the month of October, 1881, he was seized one night with an attack of illness of so severe a nature that he became apprehensive that his end might be very near. About midnight he said to his brother, David, who shared the same room with him, "I feel, David, as if I were going home." He then rose from his bed, and, opening his desk, wrote in pencil on the back of a religious leaflet, afterwards found amongst his papers, the following "testimony." In view of what he imagined might prove to be the last enemy his anxiety was to leave behind some little memorial to the faithfulness of his Covenant God. This testimony is of value from the fact that, when, a year later, the Master did call him home, the nature of his illness precluded so precise a declaration of his assurance :—

"*If before morning I should go home, this is my testimony:—'My Beloved is* MINE, *and* I AM HIS.' *Jesus is* MINE! '*I live; yet not I, but Christ liveth in me.*' '*I know Whom I have believed.*'"

CHAPTER VI.

PREPARATIONS FOR BECOMING A MISSIONARY.

TIME, ETERNITY, AND PERISHING MILLIONS OF CHINESE—STRONG ARGUMENTS WITH HIS PARENTS—LETTER TO HIS SISTER—PASSING EXAMINATIONS—LAST VISIT HOME—FINAL PARTING WITH FRIENDS—TOM'S CONVERSION—SUDDEN CONVERSIONS—INCIDENTS AT EDINBURGH.

HIS love for China slumbered not, and he had already taken steps towards preparation for the work on which his heart was set—

"Oh, how time does fly (he writes on October 4th, 1881), and we are flying with it—and *whither?* Ah, that is the question—*whither?* It flies with rapid wing onward—onward towards the judgment seat. . .

"What of the millions—the 800,000,000—of poor dark-minded heathen, who have never heard of the saving name of Jesus, who are living without hope, and without God in the world, and who, notwithstanding this, are, like ourselves, hastening onward to the judgment seat of an offended God? Awful! awful Eternity!

"'Ought we whose souls are lighted
With wisdom from on high;
Ought we to men benighted
The Lamp of Life deny?'

"I am going to ask you a question, my dear mother. Do you love Jesus enough to give one of your boys up to preach Christ Jesus to the poor heathen of China? You may say, 'Oh, he might die away out in China, and I would never see him again.' Nay but, mother, you *would* see him again. Dear mother, to assist you in coming to a settled conclusion on this matter just think of this: the holy and blessed God gave not one son out of a number, but His *only-begotten* and beloved Son that they (the heathen) and we might have life. Your boy *might* die, but Jesus *came to* die.

"'Oh, depth of love, how full, how free!
To make a way to heaven for me.'

"You know, dear mother, that I am a candidate for missionary work in the interior of China. Are you quite willing to give me up to go there at any time the Lord may call, and open the way, for me to go? Would you say, '*Even so Father*,' if I were to be called away very soon? I do not know that I shall be, but if I were would you and father be quite willing for me to go? Will father and yourself pray about it, and ask God to show you and me what His will is concerning this matter; and when we do know what His will is to give us grace to do it, for Jesus' sake? Please write to me about it. It would be so cheering and stimulating, if *(D.V.)* I should go to a foreign land to preach Christ, to know that I had the sympathy and prayers, as well as the warm love of my dear father and mother."

(To his sister, Annie.)

"4 Pyrland Road, London, N.,
December 13, 1881.

"My dearest Sister, Annie,—I received your very welcome letter yesterday, and if in one way I feel glad that you are going to a situation, yet I also feel sorry, because I know, Annie—and while I write this I feel it, oh, so much—that I am not able, nor have I been able for a long time past, to help you in worldly goods. I do not think it is at all necessary for me to tell *you*, Annie, that if I were able I would only be too glad to do so. But I can, and will, help you by prayer, and I know that our loving Heavenly Father, will both hear and answer prayer. . . .

"You know that I am staying at the Mission House of the China Inland Mission, as a candidate for becoming a missionary to China. If it is God's will, and if He has called me to the work, then I shall go to China, and if not I will not. But my own firm belief is that I shall go. Pray for me. . . .

"I have no idea how long I may have to stay here, but I do not think it will be more than a month or two. Meanwhile, with love to you all at home, I am your affectionate brother,

"Willie."

(To his Mother.)

"China Inland Mission,
6 Pyrland Road, Mildmay,
London, N., *Dec. 22, 1881.*

"My dear Mother,— . . . I think I have passed all the preliminary *exams.*, and if the doctor passes me there is every probability that within two or three months I shall *(D.V.)* be on my way to China. I do not think you need expect to see me at the New Year, because it will be the second week in January before the next Council meeting, and then I expect it will be all settled if I am to go to China, and when I may have to go. If everything goes well it is likely I will go home—*home*, did I say? Oh, dear mother, it is a long time now since I realised the import of that word. Of course all this may be set on one side at any time, so that I am leaving it all in the hands of my blessed Lord and Master. I intend to wait patiently for His time, and then by His grace and in His strength follow wherever He may lead me. Oh, may God give me help and grace to do His holy will, for Jesus' sake.

"Believe me, my own dear mother, to be your affectionate son, who desires for you and all loved ones far more than it is in his power to do or to give; but, oh, my mother, do trust Jesus."

(To his brother, Tom.)

"Pyrland Road, Mildway, N.,
Jany. 16, 1882, 3 a.m.

"My very dear Brother,—I thank you very much for the nice card you sent me. I was so very glad to get it from you, dear Tom.

"Well, Tom, I thought I should have seen you all before now, but my visit has been delayed for an indefinite period—*i.e.*, for a week or more. There will be a Council meeting on the 19th, when I hope it will be definitely settled when I am to go to China; and then I will *(D.V.)* get home, and have a short time of rest and quiet. I shall tell you everything when I get home. . . . You will hear from me as soon as I know what is to be done. Meantime, praying that God may greatly bless you all, I remain your brother

"WILLIE."

Macgregor passed his examinations satisfactorily, was approved, and in a few days afterwards arrived among his over-joyed friends in Dingwall. His brief visit will never be forgotten by them. He cared to speak of but one subject, and that subject seemed as if filling his heart with solemn and abiding joy. He associated only with those who sympathised with active Christian work. His very presence was felt to be a rebuke to lethargy and worldliness, and a help towards holy resolution. He talked much of "China and its millions," and their conversion to God, and never failed to ask for prayer on behalf of his mission to that great Empire. His demeanour was altogether fascinating and endearing; his greetings were so cordial, and he evinced so deep and Christian an interest in every one. Grace had marvellously transformed him into the image of Christ Jesus, his Lord and Master. Mr. Hudson Taylor, of the China Inland Mission, speaking (in 1887) of Macgregor to a friend remarked, "The fragrance of that young man's life is with us to this day;" and so among the friends of Macgregor in Dingwall, the fragrance of his last short visit home has not yet passed away.

The parting of Macgregor and his friends was very affecting. The aged father, bent down with infirmity, clung closely to his son, and the son showed an equally affectionate regard for his father. However it might be with the younger members of the family, the father and son knew they, at least, would not again see each other's face on earth. Macgregor's parting with his mother had already taken place, but the father resolved on accompanying him for a short distance on his way to the railway station. His strength, however, failed him before he had gone the full distance he had intended. The old man's last words, uttered with choking emotion, were words of affection and encouragement—and thus they parted. The overcome parent remained standing till the retreating figure of his son had passed out of sight, answering back farewell wavings of the hand by raising his staff and holding it aloft. The wistful gazings and falling tears of the father were embarrassing to the son.

"I know," he said to a friend who accompanied him to the station, "I shall not see my dear father again. This is one of the hardest trials I have yet had to bear."

On the station platform a number of friends had assembled to wish the young missionary God-speed. In earnest conversation with these friends he spent his last moments in Dingwall—exhorting the unconverted to yield themselves up to God, and impressing upon Christians to be true to Christ and His cause.

Before the train had yet started from the platform, all unknown to Macgregor, however, there was the first perceptible instalment of an abundant answer to his importunate prayers on behalf of his brother Tom.

Conviction had already been doing its work in the conscience, but this was not known till afterwards. In the midst of the leave-takings Tom approached a Christian young man, and a former schoolfellow, and laying his hand on his friend's shoulder, said—

"Can you meet me to-night, after business? I wish to see you very particularly."

An appointment was made and kept, the Christian friend being at once struck with a persuasion, notwithstanding Tom's avowed disbelief of revealed truth, that he was in deep soul-anxiety. Tom afterwards confessed to this same friend that while he honestly sought to be sincere in his infidelity he never felt more dissatisfied with himself than when most loudly deriding or caricaturing Christianity.

At the appointed hour that night the two young friends met, but were embarrassed till a late hour by the presence of a third person, who was, unfortunately, unsympathetic. After the departure of the unconscious intruder the embarrassment continued, and both young men walked for a time in shy silence. Once or twice the young Christian sought to draw Tom into spiritual conversation, but not successfully. At last Tom broke the silence of his own accord, but it was of the star constellations appearing overhead he spoke. They now turned their steps homeward, and the Christian friend, fully realizing the situation, and fearing the opportunity might be lost, summed up courage, and in reply to a remark by Tom, that astronomy was an interesting study, said—

"Yes; but is it not very strange that men take more interest in the study of the heavenly bodies than in the study of their Maker; and in trying to account for the existence of these bodies without God, rather than because of God?"

"No doubt;" was the reply, "and there must have been a Creator, but we can only come to a knowledge of the Unknown by reasoning from what we already know."

"But, 'Who by searching can find out God?'" asked the friend.

"You profess to be a Christian, and to know God," replied Tom, his eagerness betraying his feelings; "how is it then that you came to know God?"

"Through the revelation He has given of Himself in Christ and in His Word," was the reply, and this was followed up by an earnest personal application of the plain truths of the Gospel.

Before parting Tom thanked his friend for their conversation, and confessed that it was anxiety for his soul that made him ask for the interview. They again met on the following night, and talked familiarly to each other of the subjects of sin and the substitutionary work of the Lord Jesus Christ. After the significance and importance of believing in Christ as a personal Saviour, were pressed on his attention, Tom walked on in moody silence, and then suddenly said—

"Is that it?"

"Yes; 'Abraham believed God, and it was counted unto him for righteousness.'"

This led to closer personal dealing, and the decisive step was at last taken, and "seeing light in God's light," Tom's soul was illuminated with Heaven's brightness. Having come to an end of his own reasonings, his astonishment at the simplicity of God's way of salvation was great.

"How is it," he asked in bewilderment, "that people won't believe, *and it is so plain?*"

Are these sudden conversions permanent? Let the study of the cases of conversion narrated in the Word of God answer. The lives of the brothers William and Thomas Macgregor certainly did not belie the conclusion that where conversion is decisive, the mere fact that it may have been sudden need never be a cause for sceptical apprehensions regarding its genuineness. *Reformation* may be a slow, and tedious, and unsatisfactory process, but *regeneration* is the work of the Eternal Spirit. "For He spake, and it was done; He commanded, and it stood forth" (Psalm xxxiii. 9).

At Edinburgh Macgregor was met by Norman Ross, in whose congenial company he spent an hour or two, awaiting the departure of the London night train. They paid several short visits to Christian friends, the one rejoicing in the prospect of so soon reaching China as an ambassador of the Cross, and the other hoping against hope that, with a return of health—a hope never, however, realised—he too might yet be permitted to follow on the same grand errand.

"As the father is not able to go to China," said Macgregor to one friend, upon whom they called, "the son is going in his stead."

The allusion was to the fact that it was through Ross's instrumentality Macgregor was "begotten through the Gospel" (1 Cor. iv. 15). Ross smiled; but the ruling passion of a desire to proclaim the Gospel to the Chinese, was strong upon him up almost to the hour of death.

As illustrative of Macgregor's ardour in season and out of season, it may be mentioned that on taking his seat that night, at the Waverley Station, Edinburgh, and finding the compartment already occupied by a number of fellow-passengers, he at once boldly unfurled his colours by asking each, with much natural politeness, if he would accept one of the small books, pointing the way of salvation, which it was his practice to distribute. Handing one to a news-boy, at the carriage door, he patted him on the shoulder, saying,

"You may never be rich in this world, my little man, but if you give your heart to Jesus, your head will yet wear a crown of gold in glory!"

Sowing beside all waters, he never missed an opportunity to speak a word for Jesus, but always so genially and wisely that he seldom met with rebuffs. When, however, these were received he bore them meekly, and in compassion for those who gave them.

CHAPTER VII.

EN ROUTE FOR CHINA.

JOURNEY TO LONDON—JOY OVER TOM'S CONVERSION—GOING TO CHINA ALONE, YET NOT ALONE—COMMISSION AND MARCHING ORDERS—AN AFFECTING LETTER—LEAVING LONDON—STORMY VOYAGE ACROSS THE CHANNEL—ARRIVAL IN PARIS.

THE young missionary's first letter, after reaching London, is written in pencil, and "in haste." It is to his parents:—

"13 CROSS STREET, ISLINGTON,
Friday.

"My very dear Father and Mother,—I arrived here safely this morning at 9 o'clock, thanks to our gracious Father, who took care of me. I got to Edinburgh at 6.45 last night. . . . I went at once away to find Norman Ross, in whose lodgings I enjoyed a good tea. Dear Norman and his brother, John, nearly overwhelmed me with kindness. . . . At 10.20 p.m. I left by the night express for London. In one sense I never felt so sad in all my life as I did after parting with Tom. Poor Tom! he was so kind to me; and so also were yourselves. I never thought I loved you all so much. It is like tearing off one's limbs! However, I believe we shall all meet again through God's good hand upon us. Meanwhile pray for me, as I shall always do for you all. . . . With much love and gratitude,

"WILLIE."

What Macgregor's feelings were when he heard, before his departure from London, of the conversion of his brother Tom, we learn from the following letter:—

"[Isaiah xxvi. 3, 4.]

"2 PYRLAND ROAD, MILDMAY, N.,
"*Feby. 9th, 1882.*

"My very dear Brother,—I cannot tell you in words the joy and gladness that filled my soul when I read your letter. Oh, Tom! I am so glad that you have, by the help of God's Holy Spirit, seen your need of Jesus, and have now accepted of Him as your own personal Saviour. Oh, Tom, I have prayed and longed for this day after day. I have asked God to save both you and Jo, and now God has heard and answered in your case, and I believe that Jo will also soon be brought in. Well, Tom, I shall certainly continue to ask God to strengthen you; and *do* Tom—I ask it of you solemnly and earnestly—confess Christ openly. Do not fear men or devils. Confess Jesus. Never mind what man can do or say—trust Jesus for all that you need; and, oh, be very much in prayer. Tell God everything—mind that. And remember those words, of the Lord Jesus, in Mark v. 36, 'Be not afraid; only believe.'

"I am not to sail till the 5th of March. We are having meetings every night, so that really I have not a minute to spare. To-night we have a meeting in Exeter Hall, and to-morrow in another part of London. On Monday next we have another, of which I send you a copy of the handbill. . . .—Your brother in Jesus,

"WILLIE."

To his mother he writes:—

"Oh, how rejoiced I am to know that Tom has given himself to Jesus, and that he is now really and fully trusting the Lord Jesus as his own personal Saviour. Oh, praise the Lord for this! I am so thankful. How I did pray for Tom, and for Jo, and for all of you, and I'll continue to do so. I praise God for so gracious an answer to prayer, for I asked God, ere going home, that before I left for China He would bring to Himself both Jo and Tom. And now, bless His gracious name, He has brought in Tom; I am still praying for Jo, and I do believe that Jo will very soon be brought into the fold. Oh, may it be soon, for Jesus' sake.

"Well mother, the hour for my leaving the old country draws near. It is settled that I am to leave London Bridge Station at 8 P.M. on Wednesday, March 1. So far as present arrangements go I am to travel alone. There is no other person going with me; but, mother, the Lord is with me, and therefore all is well."

The following is copied from the fly-leaf of his pocket Bible:—

MY COMMISSION AND MARCHING ORDERS FOR CHINA.

Command—"Go ye into all the world" (Mark xvi. 15).
Orders—"Preach the Gospel to every creature" (Mark xvi. 15).
Encouragements to obedience—"Lo, I am with you all the days" (Matt. xxviii. 20);

AND,

"All power is given unto Me, both in Heaven and in earth" (Matt. xxviii. 18);

BESIDES WHICH,

"I will never leave thee, nor forsake thee" (Heb. xiii. 5);
"And the LORD, He it is that doth go before thee: He will be with thee; He will not fail thee, neither forsake thee; fear not, neither be dismayed" (Deut. xxxi. 8).

ONLY REMEMBER,

"This Book of the Law shall not depart out of thy mouth; but thou shalt meditate therein day and night, that thou mayest observe to do according to all that is written therein; for then thou shalt make thy way prosperous, and then shalt thou have good success" (Josh. i. 8).

The result of such obedience—"My Word. . . . that goeth forth out of my mouth, it shall not return unto Me void, but it shall accomplish that which I please, and it shall prosper in the thing whereto I sent it" (Is. lv. 11).

FOR,

"The idols He shall utterly abolish" (Is. ii. 18).
"But as truly as I live all the earth shall be filled with the glory of the Lord" (Numb. xiv. 20).

THEREFORE,

"Be strong and of a good courage; have not I commanded you?" (Jos. i. 9).
"Be thou faithful unto death" (Rev. ii. 10).

AND UNDER ALL CIRCUMSTANCES,

"My GRACE is sufficient for thee" (2 Cor xii. 9).

The following letter is very affecting. It was penned a few hours before his departure from London:—

"[Let not one be missing.]

"2 PYRLAND ROAD, MILDMAY, N.,
"*March 1, 1882.*

"My dearest Father and Mother, and loving Sisters

and Brothers,—I received your very kind and loving letters, and I do thank you very much for your loving words of sympathy and cheer. I know you all love me much better than I deserve. I only wish that I could prove to you that I love you all more than I ever knew until now. But I must not say more. I really cannot write to-day as I should wish. In two or three hours' time I will be leaving London, *en route* for China. I am going alone, but I have no fear. The Lord is with me. I am going to do His work in His name and strength, and He has promised that He will never leave me nor forsake me. He is faithful who has promised. So, dear mother, do not be sad at my leaving. We *shall* meet again.

"Good-bye, dear father! God, even our God, bless you; and if we never meet on earth again, *we shall meet* in *Heaven*. Good-bye, my own darling mother! God be with you: this is my daily prayer. Good-bye, dear Annie! Keep close to Jesus. *We shall meet again.* Good-bye, my dear Johannah! I am praying for you day and night. Oh! do give your heart to Jesus; then we shall meet again. Good-bye, my own dear Tom! I am praising the Lord for you. Oh, keep close to Jesus, and trust and serve Him with all your heart. (Psalm xlvi. 1-3.)

"Pray for me all of you, and write to me regularly on the first Monday of every month. With much love,

"WILLIE.

"P.S.—I leave London Bridge Station to-night at 8 o'clock.

"God bless you all. Oh! if we never meet on earth, see to it that we ALL meet in Heaven."

From an interesting diary kept by Macgregor during his journey to China (and which is reproduced in following pages), we learn in what spirits he left London, and the incidents of his departure :—

"HOTEL BURGUNDY, RUE DUPLOT,
PARIS, *March 2, 1882.*

"Left London Bridge Station at 8 o'clock last night. Eight dear brothers came with me as far as Croydon. Had a prayer-meeting in the train at Croydon. All the dear fellows stood upon the platform and sang,

"'There'll be no parting.'

"We then moved away, and I had what may prove the last sight of them on earth. Mr Markwick [an intimate friend, who had returned from mission work in China, owing to impaired eyesight], came with me as far as Newhaven. Here we found the wind blowing a perfect hurricane, and we were met with the cheering intelligence that the boat from Dieppe due at Newhaven at 9 A.M. had not then come in !

"Going on board I secured the privilege of a berth on the floor of the second cabin, after which I went on shore with Mr Markwick, and saw him into his room in the hotel, where, after commending each other to God in prayer, we parted, and I hurried on board to find that after consulting with some one in authority at the wharf the Captain had determined to go out. Soon everything moveable was fastened down, and the steward, after spreading a small rug on the floor intimated to me that my *bed* was all ready ! After I had read and committed myself to the care of Him who slumbers not nor sleeps I lay down, feeling very happy and, I trust, thankful for His sustaining grace on that —to me—eventful day.

"All was now quiet, and I thought it was just possible if I went to sleep, I would not waken till we had crossed. Vain dream. Presently the steward was to be seen flitting about the cabin, depositing a white basin at the head of each berth. This portentous preparation over he retired, and all was quiet again.

"At 12.15 we loosed from our moorings and steamed away. We had scarcely cleared the mouth of the harbour when we began to ship great seas. We tossed about and rolled dreadfully, and now the stillness of our cabin became suddenly broken by a most peculiar noise, followed by sundry low moans and strange *eerie* sounds. Just then the boat pitched fearfully, and everybody came tumbling on to the floor. Then began a scene which can be better imagined than described. Oh, the length of that night! How slowly the hours dragged along! Oh, I *was* sick, but very happy. I thought of the conversation I had with Miss Whitefield about the proposed tunnel, and the wish came sneaking into my heart that it had been finished long ago. However, morning came at last, and with it Dieppe. We all felt thankful to get our feet once more on solid ground.

"As we were very late and could not get a train for some time we went to the buffet in the station and tried to take some breakfast. I had coffee and a roll and butter, for which I paid one shilling. Everything was very nice and clean, but dear. Our train now came alongside the buffet, and we all got in. I had a companion, who was going to Paris for his holidays. I soon found out that he was not only going to Paris, but also to Heaven. He is an associate of the Young Men's Christian Association at Aldersgate Street, London, and had a note of introduction to the Secretary of the Y.M.C.A. in Paris. He knew a little French, and was of great service to me.

"I enjoyed the ride to Paris. Was particularly struck with the appearance of the trees all along the route. The branches, for a distance of ten or fourteen feet from the ground, were all lopped off, giving them a uniform, and, to me, unnatural appearance. The only birds I saw were rooks and magpies. I saw none of *our* little songsters, although I kept a good look out.

"Having reached Paris, my friend proposed to accompany me to my hotel, and I, seeing in all this the good hand of my God, consenting, we came to the Hotel Burgundy together. Here we had what we greatly needed, a good bath. Finding we had but a short time for letter-writing we set to work, and soon had our letters in the post-office. After this we set out to see Paris. My friend had a good guide-book, and with that and his knowledge of French we got along very well indeed. I shall not attempt a description of Paris. It is a beautiful city. Such fine wide streets, with rows of trees on each side. One does not wonder that the French are so proud of Paris. Trafalgar Square, London, is nothing to the Place-de-la-Boncorde, with the beautiful gardens on either side. We walked from there up to the Arc-de-Triomphe, which is a magnificent piece of architecture. We called at the Young Men's Christian Association in the Rue Mont Marche (I think that is how it is spelt). The Secretary was not in, but we spoke to a young man who said they were in a very flourishing condition. Praise God for that. It now began to rain, and being very tired, we made our way back to our hotel, and after reading and prayer together, we retired to rest, praising God for all his goodness to us."

CHAPTER VIII.

FROM PARIS TO STRAITS OF MESSINA.

A SAD SIGHT—DOING SOMETHING FOR THE MASTER BY THE WAY—IMPRESSIONS OF LYONS AND MARSEILLES—A SABBATH ON THE MEDITERRANEAN—ROMANIST AND OTHER FELLOW-PASSENGERS—PERSONAL REFLECTIONS—NAPLES, VESUVIUS, AND ETNA—PERFECT PEACE—PREACHING JESUS TO FELLOW-PASSENGERS.

TO his friends in Dingwall, Macgregor wrote from Paris, within an hour after his arrival there, expressing the same sentiments as those contained in his diary, finishing off with the words—

"Truly the Lord is going before me, and preparing everything for me. Bless His holy name."

To resume the diary:—

"HOTEL DE GENEVE MARSEILLES,
"*March 4, 1882.*

"Awoke yesterday morning [in Paris] feeling quite refreshed, and the events of the previous day seemed almost like a dream. I could not realize that I was really on my way to China, and I almost expected to hear the bell ring for prayers. Of course I did not hear it, but I did hear a knocking at the door, and upon opening it I found it was the waiter with our breakfast. That *was* real, although my dream of home was not about breakfast!

"My friend wishing to go to a different part of the city I went out by myself, and after walking about for some time (under a pouring rain all the while) I came back and went into the 'Madalene.' I was quite surprised at the number of people going in and out. As I entered I saw a large number of priests and other actors going through some ceremony. As I wished to know what it was all about I spoke to several of those who, like myself, were spectators of the scene. At last I found a young man, a Dane, who understood English, and I had a nice talk with him. He was a Protestant, and I spoke to him of the necessity of a personal dealing with God through the only Mediator, our Lord Jesus Christ. (He told me that he had been watching me for some time, and that he knew I was a Protestant.) From him I learned it was St Somebody's Day—I forget the name—but the 'idol' stands just on the right hand side as you enter the Church. I noticed that all who came in after dipping in the holy water and crossing themselves came over and prostrated themselves before this 'idol,' then rising up they gave their gifts to a woman in attendance, and she immediately lighted a small wax candle and stuck it on a stand, made for the occasion I suppose, which stood, one on either hand of the 'idol.' Oh, how my soul was stirred within me! I do believe that it was a good thing for me that I did not understand French, or I might not yet have left Paris. The 'idol' itself looked like a beautiful Christmas tree. There were also three coffins brought into the place, headed by processions of priests and others. I never witnessed such a horrible sight in my life. May God have mercy on the poor deluded people, who have for their instructors such impostors!

"Leaving the place I went back to the hotel, and after settling everything, and getting a cab, and accompanied by my friend, we drove to the Gure-de-Lyon, where we parted, hoping to meet each other, if not on earth, in Heaven. My train left the station at 2.50 p.m., and, after a comfortable journey through a very pleasant country, we got to Lyons at 6.10 a.m. Here I had some breakfast, and had time to walk about and exercise myself. We left Lyons at 7.35 a.m., and got into Marseilles at 6.40 p.m. I quite enjoyed the journey, although the carriages kept full all the way, so that I could not lie down. Having a good stock of French tracts and 'British Workmen,' I was able to do something for the Master, although I could not speak one word for Him. The people, with very few exceptions, received them gladly. Some of those who were going with me as far as Marseilles were very kind and polite to me, and by signs made me understand that they wanted to know if they could help me to get accommodation for the night. I showed them in the time-table the advertisement of the Hotel-de-Geneve. They seemed so pleased, and when we got to Marseilles conducted me to the omnibus for the hotel, offering to carry my luggage, and, after seeing me safe into the 'bus, they bowed, and we shook hands and so parted.

"The journey from Lyons to Marseilles was through a beautiful country, richly wooded and well watered. We passed several nice towns and many little villages picturesquely situated, with here and there a gentleman's chateau perched on some lofty spot, and commanding a view of the whole surrounding country; or nestled in some sheltered nook, surrounded with beautiful grounds. As we neared the coast the country got more and more beautiful. The trees were all in bloom, especially one kind, which I supposed to be the almond, with beautiful white, and, in some cases, pink blossoms. It was really lovely. At every station along the route men and women were selling boiled eggs, sweetmeats, and wine at 1 fr., or 10d, the bottle. They were nice and clean-looking people, and had none of the appearance of our hawkers. My fellow-passengers were quite astonished that I would not take any of the wine which they very freely offered me, or smoke the cigarettes they put at my disposal. Some of them I noticed drank three or four bottles of this wine before we got to our journey's end.

"Getting to my hotel I found the attendant, who speaks English, and was soon conducted to my room, away up in the top of the house—a very comfortable room indeed. As I felt very tired, after writing a short note to some friends, I asked to be woke up at 7 A.M., and to have my breakfast at 8, and, after thanking my loving and gracious Father for all His watchful care over me, I lay down to sleep feeling very happy and peaceful.

"*March 6th, 1882.*

"Out upon the blue waters of the Mediterranean with a stiff breeze blowing, every wave brings me nearer to China. Praise God.

"We left Marseilles yesterday morning at 10 o'clock

—a lovely morning, but everything hurry and bustle. Found it hard to realise that it was Sabbath morning. Going on board I made my way to the third-class cabin, and giving up my paper the steward showed me my berth, and putting my things in it, and putting my Bible into my pocket, I went away to the bows of the boat, and there, sitting down upon a sail, I opened and read the letters which dear friends had sent to me to the boat. I had quite a number—six or eight at least. The whistle now blew, and the place was quite crowded with friends taking leave of one another, but as I had no one to bid good-bye to, or even speak to (for as yet I had not met one who could understand English), I sat where I was, and taking out my Bible I spent one of the most blessed Sabbath mornings I ever remember. I felt a little lonely at first, which led me to look up to Him who hath said, 'Lo, I am with you all the days,' and I did realise, in a way that I never did before, what that meant. Oh, bless the Lord; He filled me with a joy and gladness that has not left me since.

"We have a large number of first-class passengers. Amongst them are some Priests and Sisters of Mercy. I have had a conversation with one of the priests. I find he is going to China as a missionary. He leaves me at Hong-Kong (I wish he would sooner). He shuns me now. If I go down one side of the boat he crosses over to the other side, or goes below. Some of the passengers have taken notice of it. He evidently does not like me. I do not know why, unless he has got to know something about me from the steward in our quarter. We have two Spanish ladies, and two Chinese nurses; four Spaniards, five Frenchmen, and three Englishmen, including myself. The other two are going to Yokohama, Japan. One is a young lad going out to his father, and he is in charge of the other, who, I think, is a very bad man. I have had a long talk with both of them, but the elder one thinks I am an enthusiast, and says that after a bit I will cool down, and he congratulates me on what he calls 'getting the post.' Oh, God, my God, keep me from ever growing cold, or looking upon any work in China as a 'post.' I am praying for both of them.

"On Sunday night the sea was lovely. It was almost full moon, and not a cloud in the sky, while the blue waters of the Mediterranean were calm as glass. Away on our left we could see high snow-topped mountains, which I took to be the Alps. I walked the deck until late, and strange thoughts passed through my mind as I paced to and fro alone—thoughts of home—of my past life—of all that the Lord had done for me—how He had borne with me in all my wanderings, in all my sinfulness—how He had saved me, and led me on step by step—and how unfaithful I have been to Him. The sense of God's goodness to me was crushing, and I had to do—what I do now—look away from unfaithful self to Him whose mercy and love are like Himself—infinite—eternal. Oh, I do want to be used by Him! I want to glorify Him in all things, whether on sea or land. In life and death, thine I am, oh, Lord. Thee would I serve. Oh, take and fit me. Make me a vessel meet for the Master's use, for Jesus' sake. Amen.

"*March 7th, 1882.*

"The wind blew hard all day yesterday. Quite a number of my fellow-passengers were sick, but I felt no inconvenience. I was able to take my food with a relish (this is all in answer to prayer.) The night was really lovely. Although windy, a clear sky and full moon. Retired to bed early. Awoke at 2 a.m., and looking out of the port-hole—which I can do lying in my berth—I found we were close to Naples, and half-an-hour afterwards everybody in our cabin sprung to their feet, awakened by a tremendous noise, which we found was caused by the dropping of the anchor. I thought the passengers made more noise talking away in Spanish and French than even the anchor!

"Everybody rushed on deck to see Vesuvius. And there it was, quite close at hand, great clouds rising from it, and a dull red flame at times visible through the smoke. As we have been lying here beside it all day I have been gazing at it in wonder and awe. The view from where we are just now is really grand. The city lies before us in the form of a crescent built upon a sloping ground, rising rapidly as it recedes from the shore, so that the houses seem to rise one above another, giving it a beautiful appearance. On the right hand horn of the crescent Vesuvius rises like a great sentinel, and, just opposite, on the left horn, there rises a high hill with a fortification on the top of it.

"I had often heard of the beautiful Bay of Naples. Well, it *is* beautiful, but I think the view as we sailed out of Marseilles was even more beautiful. However, I suppose that is a matter of taste.

"We left at 4 P.M. and I had got a good look at the railway, which runs up the mountain. One of the passengers allowed me to look through his glass. It seems a daring scheme.

"WEDNESDAY, *8th March, 1882.*

"Awoke this morning at five, and going on deck found that we had entered the Straits of Messina, which at the narrowest point, I suppose, to be about a mile and a-half wide. The country looked beautiful on either side, and we had a good view of Mount Etna, but the top was covered with clouds. Away on the left (the mainland) we saw a great ridge or chain of snow-topped mountains.

"*March 9th.*

"Up at half-past five this morning—my usual time since coming on board. Went on deck to see the sun rise, the wind still blowing softly. Since then it has increased to a gale, and just as I am holding on and writing this, sea after sea is breaking over us, and coming pouring along the deck. It *is* stormy, and we have two days before we sight Port Said. The noise is deafening. How sweet to know that He is with me '*now.*' Have just been reading the 89th Psalm, 8th and 9th verses, also 93rd Psalm and verse 4th. *Perfect peace.*

"*March 10th.*

"A lovely morning, the sun shining down upon a beautiful smooth sea. The storm of last night has passed away, for which all on board seem thankful. Oh, it was rough! Last night one great iron ring which was holding some ropes, snapped into four pieces, and the great big ship lay over on her side just as if she would go down. Some of the ladies were crying out, and men were shouting. The noise was deafening. I felt just then how unspeakably precious Jesus was to me; and the words which dear friends at home so often quoted to me ere leaving England, viz., 'Lo, I am with you alway,' came to me with such a sweet and comforting and cheering influence. I began to sing—

> "The Lord is my Rock, and in Him I trust—
> A Refuge in the time of storm;
> Secure whatever may befall—
> A Refuge in the time of storm.'

"I have always believed it, but now I have proved it, that in time of storm, as in calm, the Lord can and will keep in perfect peace those whose minds are set upon Him. Bless His dear name.

"To-day I have been looking over the bows of the boat, and it is lovely. The sun shining on the spray from the bows causes a beautiful rainbow, and at night when it is dark the flashes of phosphoric light from the waves are very beautiful.

"I am glad that I did not take a great big chair with me. There are numerous coils of rope set in the forepart of the ship, on which one can sit with ease, if not comfort; but as I am not confined to one part of the ship, and there are plenty seats away aft, I am never at a loss for a seat.

"As we left the Straits I took my last look of Europe, for some time I hope. We now stood out to sea and the wind rising we began to move about a little, the wind continuing to rise as the day wore on, until now it is blowing quite a gale, with the sea running high. Everybody in our quarter is lying in his berth. This is altogether different from what I had anticipated in the Mediterranean.

"Had a long conversation with two of the second-class passengers and some others who understand English. One of them, Mr F——, who is going to Shanghai, spoke in very disparaging terms of missionaries to the heathen, some of whom, he said, were better than the men who came to teach them, and we ought to convert the heathen at home first, *etcetera, etcetera.* At this they all chimed in, and I found that all who stood around were quite at one in their dislike of missionaries. However, looking up, I tried to speak faithfully and personally to each of them and preached *Jesus* unto them. Of course I came in for a good deal of sneering and scoffing, but still I am not without hope that even this feeble attempt to sow the seed may receive the blessing of God, and bring forth fruit to the glory of His holy name. On parting with them for the night Mr F——, with whom I was standing alone, put out his hand and said—

"'Mr Macgregor, I believe as firmly as you do that Jesus Christ is the Son of God, and that He died for me, but I find it so hard to do what I know to be right. I have no power over some evil habits,' *etcetera.*

"I told him of Jesus, the almighty Saviour, who could save him from *all* his sins, if he would but trust Him. He really seemed to feel it when I told him what a Saviour Jesus was to me, and bidding me good-night, he held out his hand, and said—

"'Sir, I do wish you every success in your work, and

hope that your expectations concerning China may be all fulfilled.'

"May God the Holy Ghost show him the folly of trusting to himself, or his 'filthy rags,' and lead him to look to Him who is almighty to save, and whose blood—and that alone—can make a sinner fit to appear in the presence of a holy God.

"One of the third-class passengers is confined to his bed. Poor fellow, he is dying of consumption—a young, handsome, fine-looking man, of twenty two years of age. I have been trying to make him understand me. He is a Roman Catholic, but I think he never prays, and I think he is quite careless. I am glad that I took some jam with me, as his throat is very bad, and he has nothing to relieve him. Poor fellow, he is going home to die. He gets no sympathy from others. They say it will be a good thing when he goes ashore, as he does at Aden. Whoever reads this will, I hope, pray that God may bless to his soul the reading of a tract in French, which he understands, also a 'British Workman.'

"I hope we will be at Port Said to-morrow evening, just as dear friends at Pyrland Road are praying for me. Oh, may God answer, in my experience, every prayer put up for me from that room in the name of Jesus. As I get nearer to China I feel more and more my insufficiency and unfitness for the work. Oh, God, strengthen my hands.

"This I will post at Port Said, and continue to keep a rough journal."

CHAPTER IX.

FROM PORT SAID TO COLOMBO.

A JOYFUL SURPRISE—STAY AT PORT SAID—THROUGH THE SUEZ CANAL AND THE RED SEA—COLOMBO—FALLING ASLEEP ON DECK—MARVELLOUS ESCAPE FROM SUNSTROKE—SUDDEN RECOVERY—FERVENT GRATITUDE.

"*March 14th, 1882.*

"SINCE writing my last entry I have had a joyful surprise. It was so good of the Lord to thus encourage and cheer me at so early a stage of my journey. Bless His dear name. It is just part of that goodness and mercy and love that have followed me every day since leaving home. Bless the Lord, oh, my soul, and forget not all His benefits. On Saturday morning we sighted the coast of Africa, and at half-past one P.M. we came to anchor at the mouth of the Canal, Port Said lying in all its b———I had better not say—beauty—for according to my Western ideas of beauty that element was conspicuous by its absence. However, there it was, with the bright sun shining down upon its streets and shores, crowded with swarthy forms, chiefly Arab, clad in their long flowing dresses and turbans.

Shoes or stockings they had none. We had no sooner come to anchor than we were surrounded by Arab boats all eager to take us ashore. I had been standing at the side of the ship gazing at the strange and—to me—novel scene before us, and now turned to see if any were going ashore, when, lo, there—on the deck, and not three feet from where I was—stood Brother Wallace. I could not at first believe my eyes, but sure enough there he was, looking hail and hearty, and quite sunburnt. I felt quite a thrill of delight go through me as I grasped his hand. Along with him was Mr Whitock, the only missionary here, who labours among the sailors passing through the Canal. Finding that we were to sail in two hours' time we got into Mr. Whitock's boat, and were soon rowed ashore, and conducted to Mr. Whitock's house—a nice little cottage, quite near to the harbour. Here we had prayer together, and, oh, it was to me a soul-refreshing time. We all felt it to be a time for praise and thanksgiving to our adorable Lord and Saviour, who had thus privileged us to meet each other in this strange and foreign land. After prayer I went into Brother Wallace's bedroom, and it did seem so strange to see hanging upon the wall the group—Mr. and Mrs. Broomhall and family. I was afraid I would waken up to find that I had been dreaming. It seemed so strange that just about the time dear friends were met together in dear Pyrland Road, and supplicating the throne of grace on our behalf, we were lifting up our voices and hearts to the same gracious and ever-blessed God in this little cottage in Egypt. But it was all real, even to the blessing which I am sure we all received in answer to our united prayers.

G

"Brother Wallace led me through some streets—which are a strange mixture of French cafés and Arab bazaars, with here and there a ship-chandler's shop—to a place where we purchased some fine large oranges. I have never seen such large fruit in England, and so very cheap.

"We now went on board, as they were preparing to sail. I was sorry that I had so little time with Brother Wallace; but as we could not enter the Canal after sunset, we had to go on, or wait until sunrise next morning. The rules of the Canal oblige all vessels to lie from sunset to sunrise. So we parted with the mutual prayer that God would bless us, and that in our different spheres of labour we might have grace to glorify His name, who has called us out of darkness into His marvellous light. And I also pray that God may be pleased to spare us both to meet in China, to which land I hope the Lord will be pleased to send my beloved brother.

"Mr Whitock was so very kind to me when I told him that I had no Scriptures to give away. He gave me a good supply of French Testaments and small tracts, and some Spanish tracts and Bibles, also some English papers and small books. He appears to be a dear, good man, and very earnest. May God's richest blessing rest upon his labours at Port Said.

"March 15th, 1882.

"We entered the Canal on Saturday at 5 P.M., and got to Suez on Monday at 1 P.M. It was warm as we came near Suez, but, oh, what a desert! Nothing to be seen on either side as far as the eye could reach but—sand. On Sabbath it was very hot, without a cloud in the sky. We had a splendid opportunity of witnessing that strange atmospheric illusion the 'mirage' of the desert. I was quite certain it was a real scene, for I could see the water rippling on the shore of what seemed to be a large lake, and I could see the rocks on the shore ; but we were assured by those who knew, and by natives on board, that it was all an illusion. It set me athinking of that other desert in which so many are wandering and pursuing things which, with all their seeming reality, in the end prove to be nothing but mirage. I thanked God that by the power of His blessed Spirit my eyes had been opened, and that now I look not at the 'things that are seen,' but at the 'things that are unseen, for the things that are seen are temporal, but the things which are unseen are eternal.'

"We passed several English homeward-bound ships in the Canal, and one troopship, bringing home troops from India. All were flying the yellow flag, being in quarantine.

"We are now running down the Red Sea to Aden, where we expect *(D.V.)* to be on Saturday morning. The weather is very hot. We have an awning covering the whole of the ship. As I am sitting writing this I am doing so without my waistcoat on, and perspiring freely. Not a breath of wind ! and the sea is as smooth as glass. Oh, it is glorious. I do like warm weather. I hear there is cholera at Aden. If so we will not be allowed to go ashore.

"Amongst our first-class passengers are General ——, with his lady and suit, the Marquis of ——, *etcetera*, but I have been unable to find *one* Christian, except the Priests already referred to.

"I will post this at Aden—all being well.

"*March 28th, 1882.*

"Seventeen hours' sail out from Ceylon. 'What shall I render to the Lord for all His benefits towards me?' (Psalm cxvi. 12.) This is my first entry since the 15th. The reason may or may not be seen from the diary. Anyhow I have great reason to be thankful to my Heavenly Father for all His goodness and mercy to me since then. After two days and a night of very stormy weather we got into Aden on Saturday night the 18th, and left next morning at half-past ten o'clock. It was very hot, and it looked such a desolate place—with nothing to be seen but huge rocks. Not a sign of vegetation could be observed from the ship, and very little when on shore—only a few small trees around the English Church. The place seems well fortified, and there were numbers of soldiers to be seen; but the great point of interest to strangers is the huge water tanks, which are cut out of the solid rock, and are capable of containing millions of gallons of rain water.

"Here, as at Naples and Suez, we were boarded by crowds of men selling curiosities. I never saw such a dirty, wretched-looking crowd in my life. They quite beat the natives at Port Said. They could all of them have been decently fitted out with two or three changes of raiment at any rag shop in London!

"We left Aden on Sabbath morning, and, contrary to expectation, we had a calm sea all the way to Ceylon, entering the harbour at Colombo at 8 P.M. on Sabbath, the 26th, thus completing the distance—of over 2100 miles—in eight days.

"The weather was, and is so now, very hot, and, as

we had no wind, the passengers could not sleep below at night. Everybody slept on deck—1st, 2nd, and 3rd class. As the nights were very dark it was dangerous to walk about, as men and women lay asleep all over the deck. I enjoyed it very much. Not much trouble in making my bed! just lay my rug down on the softest plank I can find, and my pillow under my head, and under the soporific influence of the engine's monotonous thud, thud, I am soon fast asleep, to be awakened by the boatswain's whistle at 4 A.M., as he calls the watch to wash the decks. All have then to go below. It's just take up your bed and walk. Woe to the poor fellow who has crept into some corner and cannot be seen, as the hose is soon at work, and is rather a rude awakener.

"On Sabbath last I came well-nigh losing my life; but thanks be unto God, who not only forgiveth all our iniquities, but also healeth all our diseases, what seemed to be a great evil my loving Father made an occasion of blessing, and of showing to me, His unworthy servant, His great love and tender mercy. It happened on this wise. About eleven o'clock A.M. I took my Bible and Mr Spurgeon's sermon for the day, and going forward sought and found a quiet spot, where I could be alone, and so commune with my Father in Heaven. I sat down upon a coil of rope, and as it was very hot I took off my hat and laid it beside me. I thought there could be no harm in doing so, as there was a good awning overhead. After reading the sermon I took the Book, and began looking up parallel passages. I was so occupied that I did not notice how time flew, until about one o'clock a gentleman came where I was and spoke to me.

Immediately on standing up I felt my head ache dreadfully, and felt quite ill, and, trembling all over, I went below. This gentleman gave me his sponge with cold water and I had my head sponged all over. I then lay down, but I soon got worse, and began to be sick. Everybody was very kind to me, suggesting this, that, and the other thing. However I rose, and kneeling down I told my Father all about it, and immediately I felt quite calm and very happy, and in spite of the significant looks and gestures of those around me I felt certain my fate was not that of being cast overboard until I reached Shanghai.

"Two of the Catholic Priests brought the doctor to me, and he ordered me to have ice to my head. During the whole of the night I was quite feverish, and I had a cloth rung out of cold water kept on my head. During the night I felt so happy that I could not refrain from singing at times. Of course this was set down for light-headedness, but, bless the Lord, it was from the heart, not the head. Towards morning I got some sound sleep, and awoke feeling quite well, though a little weak, and now I am just as well and strong as ever, if not more so. They were all surprised how well I got over it, and the steward told me that on one of their voyages a young man was sun-struck sitting in the same place in which I sat, and died in an hour and a-half afterwards. Everybody said there was no doubt if I had continued to sit a few minutes longer it might have proved fatal. There is a double awning over the whole of the after-part of the ship, a single one being of very little use with such a hot sun overhead. I suppose as my seat was rather a rough one I must have kept moving about, and so got beneath where the awnings join. I do not know, but I have all along endeavoured to be careful of not exposing myself to the sun. However this taught me a lesson. Will you join with me in thanking our God and Father for so manifestly interposing to save me from the effects of what I suppose may be called my own carelessness, and sparing me to bear witness to the riches of His grace, and serve Him in the Gospel of His dear Son amongst the millions of China? Oh, for grace to serve Him faithfully. Oh, I want to be wholly given up to Him, body, soul and spirit—*all His—only His.* Oh, how unworthy of such love, such condescension, I am. I am indeed ungrateful and full of unbelief. What a wicked heart I have, and yet goodness and mercy follow me every step. Wondrous love! wondrous love!"

CHAPTER X.

PERSONAL TESTIMONY AND EARNEST COUNSEL.

AFTER-REFLECTIONS ON ESCAPE FROM SUNSTROKE—TESTIMONY AT A MISSIONARY MEETING IN CHINA—EARNEST LETTERS TO TOM AND HIS MOTHER.

THE striking incident referred to in last chapter made a deep impression on Macgregor's mind. We find him referring to it afterwards in China. In *China's Millions*, the monthly organ of the China Inland Mission, for December, 1882, Mr. A. G. Parrott, gives an account of missionary meetings held at Gan-K'ing, in China, in which Macgregor told the story of his wonderful recovery. As the account is interesting for other reasons the quotation will be acceptable :—

"Two meetings a day were held, from seven till nine morning and evening. We numbered in all twelve persons, four of whom were ladies. The first few days were given more especially to the exposition of the Canticles. Friday, the fifth day, had been proposed as a day of fasting and prayer throughout the mission, and it certainly was a time of much blessing at Gan-K'ing. In the afternoon a meeting with the native Christians was held, and Mr. Tomalin was duly installed as pastor of the Church, in view of Mr. Pearse's approaching absence from China.

"In the evening, after a few words from Mr. Taylor, the meeting was thrown open to any who wished to speak of the way in which God had dealt with them in the past—an experience meeting which, however, I cannot attempt to describe, nor one which followed next morning. The Holy Ghost came upon us with great power, as one and another told of the wonderful way in which God had first saved them from their sins, and then led them step by step to give themselves, sometimes against their own inclinations, to the work of preaching the Gospel in China.

"The experience of one brother in this respect particularly interested us. God seems to have forced his way open before him, and compelled him to come. On the voyage out this young missionary received a severe sunstroke, and the doctors and others on board gave no hope of his recovery; but when our brother became sufficiently conscious of his position, he cast himself upon the mercy of God, and prayed that his missionary career should not be brought to such a speedy termination. He acknowledged to God that he had perhaps not exercised sufficient caution in keeping out of the burning rays of the sun, and asked forgiveness. This he did when he was alone an hour or two after the stroke. The doctor, next morning, as well as everybody else on board, was astonished to find him up and perfectly well. Instead of having to drop his dead body overboard as they expected, they had rather to congratulate him on such a speedy recovery. How many recognized the hand of God in it we cannot say, but there is no doubt whatever in the mind of our brother himself that God—JEHOVAH-ROPHI—raised him up by His own direct interposition. Immediately after prayer, the intense pain in his head decreased so rapidly that in a few hours he felt perfectly well, and, indeed, *was* perfectly well.

"On Saturday morning we concluded with a meeting more especially for prayer. For nearly two hours prayer continued without a minute's intermission. The prayers were pointed and powerful, everyone realized the presence and power of the Spirit of God upon us, and much liberty in prayer was the result. Prayer for the remainder of the seventy additional labourers, for whom more than sixty of us are banded together to pray daily, was specially definite and emphatic, and we are more than ever determined never to cease crying to the Lord of the Harvest till we see 'the seventy' thrust forth into His harvest. Some wonder why we ask for 'seventy.' We can only here say the work needs seventy times 'seventy,' and believe that in these days nothing is too hard for the Lord."

The following letters, written by Macgregor on board ship, may appropriately find a place here :—

(To his brother, Tom.)

"My very dear Tom,—Just a line to encourage you in your daily holy war against the world, the flesh, and the devil. I know that you are just in the place where you will be tempted and tried, and where, I am sorry to think, you will see much cold-hearted and luke-warm Laodicean profession. Oh, Tom, be much in prayer, and never mind what men may say to you. Strive after holiness, after entire sanctification. When you discover that your heart is full of sin do not be discouraged. It is because God's Holy Spirit is shining into your dark heart. Thank God that He has revealed it to you, and put it *all* away; and ask Him to cleanse you from all sin. Before it can, or will, be cleansed He will show you that it is there, and what a black, foul thing it is. This will humble you, and make you hate self and mourn before Him; but never let it discourage you. . . . Never, never believe the devilish doctrine that you must expect to be always falling. It is a lie, and a slander on the almighty Saviour, who can keep us, if we only trust Him. I have not time to write more, and the ship is rocking about. Good-bye, my own dear Tom. Keep near to Jesus."

(To his Mother.)

"S.S. DJEMNAH,
RED SEA, *March 16, 1882.*

"My very dear Mother,—Although I have written to Tom, yet I know you will be pleased to have a letter yourself from 'Willie.' God bless you, my mother. I am sure that you feel my leaving home more than you have said; but I also feel that, believing God has indeed called me to this glorious work, you are quite willing that I should go and

"'Tell out among the heathen
That the Lord is King!'

"My prayer continually is that God would give us

grace not only to be reconciled to His holy will in all things, but also to rejoice to do His will, even should it be at the sacrifice of all our comforts, ease, and pleasure. My dear mother, unless in doing the will of our gracious Lord and Master in this sinful world we are willing to sacrifice and deny ourselves, our service is not of much account. As you will have seen by my diary I have had up to the present a very prosperous and happy voyage. Thanks be unto our loving Father, who continually watches over us. We are at the present moment running down the Red Sea at the rate of three hundred miles a day. The weather is very, very hot, and we never see a cloud in the sky—nothing all day but the hot sun. We are going due south, and so, of course, it is getting warmer still. I am sitting in a thin alpaca suit and perspiring freely. Last night we were all lying on the top of our beds with the port holes open. My health is very good, bless God.

"Yesterday and to-day I have been much interested watching shoals of beautiful flying-fish, which rise out of the sea at the ship's side, and fly along the surface of the water ever so far. Lovely little things they appear to be. I would very much like to catch one; but at the speed we are going it is impossible. . . .

"We expect to be in Aden on Saturday morning. The run down the Red Sea from Suez to Aden is about 1400 miles. We shall remain in Aden twenty-four hours, and then go right out to sea, not again seeing land until we get to Ceylon, a distance from Aden of over 2100 miles. When we get there our journey will be about half over. . . .—Your ever loving and affectionate son,

"WILLIE."

In a letter addressed to the family from the Straits of Malacca, on April 1st, he says—

"I hope *(D.V.)* that in seventeen days more I shall reach Shanghai. . . .

"Dear Tom,—Give my love to ——. I shall write him from China. Love also to ——, and all the others. . . . Dear Tom, I am praying for you, day and night. May God bless you, and keep you. Trust Him fully, Tom."

CHAPTER XI.

DIARY RESUMED—CEYLON TO CHINA.

IMPRESSIONS OF CEYLON—IN A BUDDHIST TEMPLE—THE HOLY BOOKS—PREACHING JESUS TO BUDDHIST PRIESTS—IN THE TROPICS—MAN OVERBOARD—A SABBATH IN SINGAPORE—SIGON—SETTING HIS EYES ON CHINA—EUROPEAN INFLUENCE A CURSE TO THE HEATHEN—WELCOME AT SHANGHAI—ARRIVAL AT GAN-K'ING.

TO resume Macgregor's diary :—

"As we had twelve hours at Point de Galle I went on shore, and as there was quite a large party of us we engaged a native guide, who showed us all over the European part of the town. But my friends very soon got tired of walking about, the day being very hot, and they proposed adjourning to the 'Oriental Hotel.' Of course I did not go, and I was very glad to get away, as I wanted to see the country and the natives, and not European things and people. So they paid the guide, and then I engaged him, and as he could speak English very well I told him to lead me out into the country, and then I asked him if there was a native village near. He said there was, and he led me to it, through a thick wood of cocoa-nut trees. The houses I found were built with stakes and a kind of wicker-work and matting made from the cocoa-nut fibre. The roof is covered with the huge leaves of the plantain tree. They were not built in rows, and no attempt seemed to be made to form streets—just a house here and there built against a cluster of trees.

"I shall not attempt to describe the scene. It was simply glorious—not a barren spot to be seen. Every inch of ground was covered with vegetation in rich profusion. There were cocoa-nut, orange, and banana trees, all laden with fruit, pine-apple, mangoes, bread-fruit, and I know not how many other kinds of fruit trees, all growing in abundance, besides which the ground is covered with beautiful flowers, and the air laden with delicious perfume. I thought of and sang Heber's beautiful hymn—

"'From Greenland's icy mountains,
From India's coral strand,
Where Afric's sunny fountains
Roll down their golden sand;
From many an ancient river,
From many a palmy plain,
They call us to deliver
Their land from error's chain.

"'What though the spicy breezes
Blow soft o'er Ceylon's isle,
Though every prospect pleases,
And only man is vile?
In vain with lavish kindness
The gifts of God are strewn,
The heathen in his blindness
Bows down to wood and stone.

"'Can we whose souls are lighted
With wisdom from on high,
Can we to men benighted
The lamp of life deny?
Salvation, O salvation!
The joyful sound proclaim,
Till each remotest nation
Has learnt Messiah's name.'

'Every prospect' is not only pleasing but enchanting. I was escorted all over the place by troops of children, all of them begging me to give them something. Some were quite naked, others had on what I suppose was intended to represent a shirt. But beautiful children they were notwithstanding—with such intelligent faces and lovely eyes.

"I sat down under the trees, and they all stood in a circle round me, and I spoke to them, my guide acting as interpreter. There were three or four elderly persons also standing amongst them. Oh, how my heart yearned over the dear children. Poor little mites, they are growing up in ignorance of the loving Saviour who said, 'Suffer the little children to come unto Me, and forbid them not.'

"After I had refreshed myself with some oranges and bananas, and drunk some cocoa-nut milk I moved on again.

"My guide, I found, was a Buddhist, and he offered to bring me to the Buddhist Temple. On our way we came to the Mahommedan Mosque. It is a small hall with an outer court, where there is a pool of water full of holy fish. Before going into the Mosque each person goes to the pool and washes his feet and hands, his mouth and teeth. In fact, outwardly he must be thoroughly clean before going in to worship. I thought of Matthew xxiii. 25, 26, and also 1st John i. 7. Going on further we came to the temple, hid away among the trees—a very nice looking building.

"Entering I saw the idols with the morning offerings of flowers, *etcetera,* still before them. I cannot describe to you my feelings at the sight. There were three priests in attendance—one old man with a beautiful face, and two younger ones. At my request the old man brought out the two holy books. The writing is on palm leaves, held together by string, like a Venetian blind. As I held them in my hand I asked the old man who the writer of them was, and where did they come from. He said they were given by God, but I could get no satisfactory answer as to the manner, further than that some one had been taken up to Heaven, and when he came back he wrote them. I found his tale very simple and childish. I did not argue with him, but as we had a crowd around us I asked him if he would listen to my doctrine. He said he would, and I began to preach *Jesus* unto them, my guide interpreting as I went on. They all listened attentively, and the old man said it was all good, and that he would like if I could come again and talk more about it. He said he liked me very much, and he was sorry he could not understand English.

"As it was now time for me to return I shook hands with the poor old man, telling him that I hoped to meet him in Heaven. I came away praying that the Lord would own and bless the few words I had spoken in Jesus' name. After a good walk I got back to our boat, and was rowed on board, tired but very happy. My heart was full of joy, although saddened by what I had that day seen and heard. My guide told me that there are four Churches at Point de Galle, viz., Roman Catholic, English, Wesleyan, and Presbyterian. I saw the Roman Catholic Church. It is a magnificent building. I also saw the Wesleyan Chapel. It is a nice, large, plain building.

"May God prosper every effort put forth in Ceylon to rescue the perishing.

"We are now running down to Singapore, where we hope to be on Sabbath *(D.V.)* the 2nd day of April. There I hope to see the Rev. Mr Grant. I am in excellent health and very happy. Bless God for all His goodness to me.

"I will post this at Singapore.

"*April 4th, 1882.*

"We have had a good passage across from Point de Galle to Singapore. Two days out from Ceylon we picked up a Chinese junk, with sixteen hands on board. They had been blown off the land in a gale, and were drifting about, not knowing where they were. They had no food on board. We towed them within sight of land, and then left them, having supplied their needs.

"Early on Friday morning we entered the Straits of Malacca. We are now really in the tropics. Every little island we pass—and there are hundreds—is covered, and even bare rocks—or rather what in other places would have been bare rocks—are here covered with green. We have high hills on either hand of us, and they are covered to their very summits with rich vegetation.

"On Saturday afternoon we had quite a sensation. Running down under full steam suddenly there was a cry—'Man overboard!' What a rush of passengers and crew! Life buoys were tossed overboard and the engines reversed; but, before we could turn round and steam after him, we had left the man quite a mile behind. Being a good swimmer he managed to get hold of a buoy, and so supported himself until a boat was lowered and he was taken on board. I felt so thankful when I saw him brought on deck, as I was told that the sea all around there is swarming with sharks.

"We got to Singapore at half-past three P.M., on Sabbath, April the 2nd, and all my fellow-passengers immediately hurried on shore, and getting into 'garries' (a kind of cab) set off for the town, which is some miles distant from where we anchored. I waited on board for some time, thinking that Mr. Grant or some one from him would meet me, as I knew that Mr Baller had written to him telling of my coming. I went on shore after dinner, and made inquiries about him; but nobody, not even a policeman to whom I spoke (a Malay) knew anything of him. Being the Sabbath-day, I determined not to take a 'garry' but walk on, and make inquiries for Mr. Grant or some Protestant place of worship. I did so, but found neither, and as it was now dark (half-past six o'clock), I abandoned the idea of seeing him that night, and turned my steps toward a sort of Chinese village I had already passed through. I had not gone far when I passed a European, to whom I spoke, and found he was a sailor returning from a meeting which a Miss Cook had been holding in the Sailors' Home. He was pleased when I asked him if he were a Christian. He said he was, and praised the Lord like a real Methodist. We spent a nice hour together, and then parted, expecting to meet again at—*Home!*

"Next morning I went on shore early (about six o'clock), and going up to the town I, after some difficulty, found Mr. Hocquerth, Mr. Grant's helper. He was very glad to see me, and very kind. I went to his house first, and had some refreshments. Then we went to Mr. Grant's house; but as Mr. Grant was away at Penang, I saw only Mrs. Grant and family. I spent a very nice time with Mr. Hocquerth in talking over his work—its joys and sorrows. It is very trying work at this place. Singapore is a beautiful place indeed, and it might be said of it as of Ceylon—'only man is vile.' Mr. Hocquerth came with me to the ship, and, after commending each other to the Lord and to the word of His grace, we parted. They were not expecting me till the P. and O. boat came in, as they heard that I was coming out with Mr. and Mrs. John, and in this belief they were confirmed by seeing in the list of passengers by the P. and O. boat the name of a 'Macgregor' going to Shanghai. It would be well were they to know definitely when anyone is coming through, as it is a treat to them to see a fresh missionary coming out. They told me that by not letting them know, so that they could meet us, we deprived them of a great pleasure. Mr. Hocquerth is a very earnest man, and he would like an interest in the prayers of Pyrland Road.

"We left Singapore at 11 A.M. on Monday the 3rd, got to Sigon on Wednesday at 3 P.M., and left next day (Thursday) at 3 P.M. for Hong-Kong. Sigon is, I have been told, a very unhealthy place, and I can easily understand how that should be, as it is surrounded by swamps and rice fields. From the time we entered the river till we reached the town—a distance of forty-nine miles—we were passing through nothing but swamps. I like the way in which the town is laid out, but it is fearfully hot on shore. Being a French colony, of course everything is French. I went into a large new building and found it was a Roman Catholic Cathedral. Everywhere I go I see swarms of Roman Catholic priests and nuns. The East is full of them. Would to God that those who have the truth, and who by it have been made free, were as zealous for their blessed Lord, and as willing to consecrate themselves and all they have to His service. It is strange—very strange!

"*April 12th, 1882.*

"From Sigon to Hong-Kong we had it very rough, the wind blowing quite a gale. I was told it was the last blow of the N.E. monsoon, ere it changes, as it does this month, to the S.W. We got into Hong-Kong harbour at 7 A.M. on Monday the 10th, and we left yesterday (the 11th) at 3 P.M. I was quite disappointed with the island of Hong-Kong; but I cannot describe to you my feelings when I gazed upon the high hills opposite, as I was told these were in China proper! I went below and thanked God that He had brought me thus far in safety, and that now with my very eyes I beheld China! Oh, may God grant that every hour I spend in China may be to bring glory to His great and holy name!

"The island of Hong-Kong is almost destitute of vegetation—nothing but huge granite rocks and bare peaks. The town itself is in a sheltered position on the southern slope of a range of high hills running the entire length of the island. The town runs along the seaside from east to west for about two and a-half miles; but has no width except in the centre, where it ascends the slope of the hill to a considerable height. This hill is called Victoria Peak, and rises at the back of the town to a height of—I should say, judging roughly—1000 feet. I saw all that was to be seen in Hong-Kong—the park, a very nice one, and the 'Happy Valley' Cemetery, where so many Europeans sleep to that great day. I found the Basle Mission, but Mr. Lechler was away up at Canton. I saw Mrs. Lechler and several other members of the Mission. They were very kind to me. They seem to be doing a good work here. We went into the schools and saw the young girls at work—some reading, and others writing. They look such intelligent children, and although kept by the Mission they do everything for themselves—cook their own food, and do their own washing. There cannot but be fruit from such an effort to rescue the dear children. While I was there a gentleman came in whom I had seen at our meeting at Pyrland Road. He is out here from the American Bible Society. He has been in Shanghai, but has come down here to try to do something. His name is A. Anderson. He was in London from September till November last year.

"He saw me on board, and I left him, feeling rather discouraged at things in Hong-Kong. It is sad, sad beyond expression, to hear the same tale from the lips of every missionary since leaving England, viz., the Europeans are a curse to the heathen. Mr. Anderson told me he could scarcely sell a book. The Government will not suffer any mention of religion in the schools. Nay more, they warned the teachers against using books having anything relating to God or religion in them. And then all the European merchants keep their servants working all day on Sabbath, and laugh at missionary effort. I am thoroughly ashamed of my country, and I shall be glad when I get into Chinese dress.

"SHANGHAI, *April 17th, 1882.*

"Oh, magnify the Lord with me, and let us exalt His name together. Praise the Lord, I am at last in China! I left Hong-Kong on Tuesday the 11th, and got into the mouth of the river on Friday evening. Finding that the steamer would have to lie there all night I determined to go up with the steam launch which came for the mail bags. I did so and was landed at the French settlement at 7 p.m. I cannot describe to any one what my feelings were as we ran up the river to Shanghai. Finding no one awaiting me I got a coolie to carry some of my things, and started off in the dark to try to find Mr. Dalziel. Having no address this will appear ridiculous to any one who knows Shanghai. However, after a little while of wandering about I found the Mission House, and received a very hearty welcome to China from Mr. J. H. Taylor, Mr. and Mrs. Dalziel, Mr. and Mrs. Douthwaite, Mr. Cameron, and Mrs. Cardwell. Some had gone to meet me but had missed me. I *did* get some hand-shakings!

"This is a large city, walled all round. One of our places is just by the North Gate; the other at the West Gate. I had better not try to describe what the city is like internally, but in the widest street by stretching out your hands you can almost touch both sides of it. However, everything is much better than I expected to see when I came here, and I like the place very well.

"GAN-K'ING.

"On Wednesday, the 19th, Mr Taylor decided to send me to Gan-K'ing for the present. So having to leave Shanghai at midnight Mr Cameron and I went out shopping, and having purchased a complete suit of native dress, and being divested of my superabundant hair, or rather having had it removed from the front of my head, I was soon transformed in dress into a quiet, decent-looking Chinaman. I may here say I like the native dress exceedingly well.

"Mr Cameron and I having bade farewell to Mr. Taylor and others left Shanghai at midnight, and next morning, on going out of our cabin, I found we were steaming up the Yang-ts'i-Kiang—a magnificent river. The scene was beautiful as we sailed up, passing cities, towns, and islands. At Chin-Kiang we met Mr. and Mrs. Tomalin, who came on with me to Gan-K'ing. Mr Cameron returned to Shanghai, and I was sorry to lose his company—he is such a nice good fellow. We arrived at Gan-K'ing on Thursday, and received a hearty welcome from all the missionaries here—Brother Prothero shouting 'Glory' as a Methodist only can. We *did* have a praise meeting! For the first few days I was very unwell, but am now quite well and strong, and very, very happy. Oh, bless the Lord."

CHAPTER XII.

IN CHINA—FIRST IMPRESSIONS, AND PROSPECTIVE WORK.

GAN-K'ING—STUDYING THE LANGUAGE—ADOPTS THE CHINESE DRESS—LETTERS TO FELLOW-LABOURERS IN LONDON—FIRST IMPRESSIONS—CHINESE SUPERSTITION AND IDOLATRY—EXCEEDING JOYFULNESS—WORDS OF CAUTION—LAST APPEAL TO YOUNGEST SISTER—HOW TO LEAD MEETINGS—MEETING WITH MR. HUDSON TAYLOR—PROSPECTIVE WORK, AND THREATENED DANGERS.

"PRAISE the Lord, I am at last in China!" The holy and joyful enthusiasm of the young missionary knew no bounds. His first letter home (dated April 26, 1882) is addressed to his mother:—

"GAN-K'ING.

"My dearest Mother,—I am sure that you are again longing to hear something about me. Well, dear mother, God has been very good to me, and brought me to China in safety. I got to this city on Thursday last, the 20th, and since then I have had three days' suffering from my old friend, neuralgia; but thanks be to my Heavenly Father, He has quite restored me again,

This is a large city, situated 400 miles into the interior. It is the "fu," or capital, of the province of Gang-Whey. I came up here by steamer. . . . The Yang-tsie or Yang-tze is a magnificent river. 900 miles up from Shanghai it is about ten miles broad. I am not to stay long here; I am going about 1500 miles farther in, to the south-west.

"I have secured a teacher, and have begun studying the language—and, oh, it *is* a language!! But I know the Lord has not sent me to China to see the country, but to preach the Gospel, and I cannot do that till I have learned the language. So I know He will help me to acquire it.

"There are no foreigners here but ourselves, viz., three gentlemen, and four ladies. I do wish you saw things as they are here. It is of no use my attempting to describe them just now. Everything is quite two or three thousand years behind time. . . .

"I am in the Chinese dress fully, from pig-tail to boots, or rather shoes—or in Chinese language, from 'p'ien-tsï' to 'a-tsï.' I have also been 'christened' with a Chinese name. . . .

"Kind love to dear father. Tell him to pray always for me. You know not how much I need it. . . .

"WILLIE.

"I am very happy indeed in China."

(To Mr. W——, London.)

"GAN-K'ING CHINA,
"*May 12, 1882.*

"My very dear brother W—— . . . Doubtless you have already heard of my safe arrival, and I am sure, my dear brother, that you have already joined with me in returning thanks to our loving Heavenly Father, who so graciously cared for me all the way out to this far-away land. Oh, bless the Lord, I would indeed be ungrateful if I did not praise Him with all my heart. Brother, I have proved it: the Lord has indeed blessed me since leaving home—blessed me an hundredfold more than ever I have been in England. I feel this so much at times that I often think the Lord is preparing me for some strange, and, perhaps, trying circumstances through which He is to lead me. Amen, Lord, all I ask is grace to serve Thee faithfully even unto death, that I may in life and death glorify Thy holy name. 'For me to live is Christ; to die is gain.' . . .

"We are a very, very happy party indeed at this station. We do have some good times even here. Brother Prothero and I have been making the place ring again with some grand old Methodist hymns. Oh, it is glorious! I wish you were out here, for you are much needed.

"Do not mistake me when I write so much about what the Lord has done and is doing for me. There is another side to all this, and an awfully real side it is. I shall not attempt to picture to you all that I have already seen of that foul thing idolatry. It is far worse than ever I dreamed of. Just think of it, the other night I was startled by hearing loud and plaintive cries almost underneath our window, and on looking and listening, found these proceeded from men who were going about with lights seeking the soul of some sick person, and inviting it to return home. . . . Then these last few nights, both before and after going to bed, just close beside us, we heard the beating of gongs, and the chanting of prayers over some one who had just died, while a strong scent of burning incense came in at the windows. Add to this the continual noise of fireworks, being let off to frighten evil spirits, and keep off evil influences. All this is to be seen and heard at our very doors. Oh, it is awful! I have been into some of the temples here, and, oh, brother, it makes my heart ache every time I see these horrid figures—even the outside of the buildings where they are kept. Oh, the misery and wretchedness of the people! Sin, filth, and wretchedness abound on every hand. We have had as many as three cases of opium-poisoning in one day—miserable men, tired of life, and wishing to escape from it (and no wonder). I am sure that if Christians at home could only see and hear for themselves they would not, nay, could not be so indifferent to China's great need. . . .

"I do not expect to remain here very long, but I hope to go west. Will you join with me in asking the Lord to make my way plain with regard to my future sphere of labour. . . .

"We are praying the Lord to send out many more labourers, but really I do not think the Council can err on the side of over-caution in dealing with candidates. It is absolutely necessary that all who come to China should first count the cost. . . .

"Pray for me, and continue to believe me to be ever your affectionate brother in Jesus' love,

"Wm. M. Macgregor."

To another fellow-worker he writes on the same date (May 12):—

"Ps. xxviii. 7; Ps. xvii. 14. . . . Also pray for poor China. Oh, my brother, had you but seen and heard all that I have since coming here, it would, I am sure, cause you, as it has done me, the better to appreciate the privileges of having been born in a land of Christian light and liberty, and of having been trained from our youth to know God's Holy Word. . . .

"This letter leaves me well in health, and as happy as it is possible for me to be down here below."

To another he writes, also on the same date:—

"Ps. xxxvii. 4, 5. . . . And now, dear brother, the desire of my heart has been given to me, and I am really in China. Oh, hallelujah! My heart is full of joy unspeakable. I never felt more certain that the Lord has called me to the work than I do just now; and, God helping and strengthening me, I mean to spend and be spent for Him in China. But let me tell you, dear brother, there is no romance in missionary life and work here. Quite the contrary, and without the firm conviction in your heart that you had been really called to the work your life would, in all probability, be a very unhappy one. And, my brother, be sure you count the cost ere you come to China. I do not want to frighten you, but I do wish, as I love you, to impress this on your mind. . . . But if He has called you, dear brother, come, and you will see how God can and will bless you far above the utmost you have dared to hope for or expect. Pray for me, dear brother, I need it."

(Last letter to his sister, Johannah.)

"GANG K'ING, CHINA,
June, 1882.

"My very dear sister, Jo,—As I am writing home, and I know you will not be at home to hear my letter, I just send you a few words, all to yourself. . . .

I have now got fairly settled down, and am wearing the full dress, not forgetting the all-important pig-tail! I am sure you would laugh if you could see me. You would not know me. I like the dress very much, only my hair is so short, and, of course, I have to wear false hair in my tail, which reaches almost to my heels. It is very warm here, and daily getting warmer. This will be a trying summer for me, being my first in China; but our dear Lord Jesus, who is with me, knows it all, and as He sent me here, I know He can and will give me all needed strength.

"Dear Jo, I hope you will not be angry with me for asking you again *if you have yet given your heart to Jesus.* My darling sister, oh, do, *do*, and make us all happy. I shall say no more, but just ask you to read St. John iii. 16-18, and 36; John vi. 32-37. I am praying for you, my dear, dear sister. Oh, do ask Jesus to show you the meaning of these precious words. Then you *can* and *will* pray for me. . . . With much love, dear Jo, I am your loving brother,

"WILLIE."

To a Christian worker seasonable advice is thus given:

"And now let me say a word about your open-air work. Need I say how happy I am in the thought that you are labouring for souls in England while I am doing the same in China. . . . I am so glad you lead the P.S. meeting. Thank God for this, but see to it that you allow the Holy Spirit to lead you. If so you need not fear leading any meeting. Beware of the devil, and beware of self, and you need not fear man. . . .

"If you feel lonely, dear brother, remember Jesus is with you. Live for Him, live with Him, live in Him, and let Him live in you, so shall you be happy, useful and glorifying to Him."

(To his Parents.)

"GANG-K'ING, *July 3, 1882.*

"My very dear Father and Mother,— . . . I am sure that even now, if you could call me back from China you would not do it. I am sure you look upon it all as I do myself—that God has conferred a great honour upon our family by choosing me, and sending me forth to be a witness for Him, and to serve Him in the gospel of His grace, in this dark and distant country. . . .

"Last week we had a small conference of missionaries at this station—or rather of a few from other stations within a radius of a few hundred miles around. They came to meet the director of the Mission, who is also the founder of it—Mr. Hudson Taylor, M.D., F.R.G.S., Oh, he is a darling man: I have never seen or heard of one like him. He is such a dear, good man—I do love him. Well, I had one or two long interviews with him about my future sphere of labour, and I told him, as I had previously done at Shanghai, of my desire to go, so soon as I can speak the language and have gained a little experience, to the, at present, unoccupied and dark province of Ruang-se, in the extreme south of China. . . .

"I do not know how many millions of inhabitants this province possesses, but for size, it is like England. Just think of it—millions who are born, brought up, and die, worshipping idols, never hearing of God or of the Lord Jesus Christ—not even having a word in their language to clearly express the idea of a God—having no word for 'love,' no word for 'sin,' *etc.*—living without God, and dying without hope. Oh, it is awful! Well, Mr. Taylor, believing it is the Lord who has laid it upon my heart, has set me apart for that province. So in God's own time I hope to have the honour of beginning work in that distant province; but in the meantime Mr. Taylor has asked me to go to the help of a dear brother, the Rev. G. Clarke, who has travelled a great deal in China, and has lately opened a station in the povince of Yü-nan, away on the south-west corner of China. The station is in a large city, Ta-li-fu. It is the most distant station in the interior, being on the borders of Burmah. Mr Clarke is there all alone with his wife—two brave soldiers of Jesus. Mr. Taylor thought that as they speak the same dialect as at Ruang-se, it would be the best place at which I could study the language for a year, while at the same time I would be a comfort and help to Mr. and Mrs. Clarke. Believing this to be God's will concerning me, I have decided to go, and hope to start as soon as the great heat is over, which will probably be about the beginning of September. I am to be escorted by Mr. Cameron, one of the greatest travellers China has ever seen. . . . We expect to get there about Christmas time. The first five or six hundred miles we can do by steamer up the great river Yang-tse, after which we will take native boats for a month or six weeks; then we will go overland for the next six or eight weeks.

"The journey will be one full of danger and difficulty, but the Lord is our Keeper. I want you to pray for me—for us—continually, and He who is the hearer and answerer of prayer—He, whose we are, and whom we serve—will hear, and will bring us to our destination in safety. Oh, it is a good thing to have the Lord of Hosts as our Captain going before us, and also bringing up the rear. Read the 91st Psalm, also the 27th and 62nd. If God be for us, who or what can hurt us? Well, dear parents, this is the human side of it: whether or not it will come to pass *He* alone knows whose knowledge is like Himself—infinite. But, oh, it is sweet to know and feel that our blessed Saviour is with us, on sea and land, by day and night, always, and under all circumstances. Oh, *we are safe anywhere with Jesus.* Peter walked on the foaming billows *with Jesus;* Shadrach, Meshach, and Abed-nego were quite unhurt in the midst of a great fiery furnace *with Jesus;* Daniel in a lion's den, Jonah in the whale's belly, Joseph in a dismal prison-house, were all safe, all happy, all blessed—why? Because *with Jesus;* and shall William Macgregor be an exception? Nay, a thousand times no! I am willing to go anywhere with Jesus. . . .

"I am going to write a long letter to Tom, all to

himself, next time. . . . With much love, I am, darling father and mother, your ever loving and praying son,

"WILLIE."

CHAPTER XIII.

HEAVENWARD AND HOMEWARD.

ANYWHERE WITH JESUS—GROWING SANCTIFICATION—HOT WEATHER—THE LORD JESUS MORE THAN COMPENSATING FOR ALL SUFFERING—PROGRESS IN THE LANGUAGE—A DEVASTATING FLOOD—HOLY GHOST POWER THE ONE REQUISITE FOR MISSIONARIES—A LAND WITHOUT SABBATHS—JOYFUL ANTICIPATION OF GOING TO KUANG-SE—THOUGHTS OF FRIENDS AND HOME—ONLY FOR JESUS—FOREIGN DEVILS—HIS LAST LETTER—DILIGENCE IN STUDY—POSTSCRIPT COUNSEL.

THE long and dangerous journey referred to in Macgregor's last letter was never undertaken. The Master had other purposes in view. "*I am willing to go anywhere with Jesus.*" He knew not, when he penned these words, in how short a time he would be "*with Jesus.*" His love for China was not ephemeral. His devotion to the cause that brought him to that great heathen country grew as the months passed. His love for his friends at home suffered no decrease, but his love for Jesus increased mightily. There was much to discourge and dishearten, but his joy in Jesus abounded all the more abundantly. The remaining letters make this plain. They are now nearly exhausted, but their ring is even clearer than any that have preceded. These letters, which are quoted at some length, give pictures of Chinese life, and show some of the difficulties encountered in evangelizing China:—

"WU-HU, *August 12th, 1882.*

"My dear brother Tom,—Please forgive my writing you with pencil, for I am out on a short journey, and have not pen and ink with me. Your last letter from home I received ere I left Gan-K'ing, and when *(D.V.)* I get back again, I shall write you about the books, and what I have studied; but just now you will please excuse me, as I only write in case father and mother and all of you might be anxious to hear from me. Let me at once say that I am very well in health, although this has been a very trying summer, and the hottest has yet to come. Just fancy my sitting quite still all day at my studies, with nothing on but a white pair of cotton *paun-jammas,* as they are called, and a very thin jacket, with wide sleeves, and very loose; no stockings, but the bare feet slipped into loose shoes. This is my toilet, and with every window and door open, I am soaking wet, as if in a Turkish bath. At night often the glass does not move, and you lie on a kind of bamboo mat, with a handkerchief and a fan, while mosquitoes are buzzing about and stinging you; add to this the hundreds of all kinds of queer insects, large and small; and sometimes you may have to turn up your bed and search your room in case of snakes, scorpions, or centipedes being about. You may think this terrible, but it is the case in hundreds of stations in China, especially in the south and west. While this is all true, we are nevertheless as happy as we can well be. Of course where our stations are in the centre of a large city there are not quite so many of these unwelcome visitors. This is something of the romance of missionary work in the interior of China!

"I shall say nothing about many other things which are far greater hardships than those I have mentioned; but Tom, I do say this, *that if things were ten thousand times worse than they are, yet I would gladly, joyfully serve the Lord Jesus in this land.* He Himself far more than makes up for all these things, and He is, oh, so good and kind to me in China. Praise His dear name! I have had a good deal of neuralgia and other ailments since coming to China, but these are nothing in comparison to the benefits with which my blessed Saviour daily loads me.

"Believing a change would do me good, and help me in getting accustomed to the Chinese voice, I have come out with a dear brother on a short journey to two of the out-stations from Gan-K'ing. The names of these places are Wu-hu and T'ai-p'ing-fu. Both are large cities. The work at each station is in charge of a native evangelist or pastor, who preaches every day to the people in our chapel. We have been to T'ai-p'ing-fu, and are on our way back. We expect to be in Gan-K'ing next week.

"I am getting on with the language, and am able to talk a little.

"The great river Yang-tsï-Kiang has this year risen to an unprecedented height; and, breaking over hundreds of embankments, has flooded the whole country for hundreds of miles, sweeping away entire towns and villages. Thousands of persons have been drowned, and thousands more have been rendered homeless. Standing on the top of a little hill here, as far as the eye can reach it is all one sheet of water, with boats sailing inland for miles over the tops of trees and houses, and over what only a week or two ago were large villages with their gardens and rice-fields. The scene of desolation is fearful—dead bodies of men, women, and children floating about, mingling with those of cattle, sheep, pigs, &c., and all decomposing in the water. Oh, it is awful!

"Poor China! poor China! Dear Tom, there are millions of people in this land, who are miserable and wretched, having no joy in their lives, and no hope for the world to come! Oh, pray for China, Tom, that the people may see the absurdity and sin of worshipping their idols, and learn to love and worship the one true and living God. The water comes and sweeps away themselves and their gods, and yet they cling to them, and burn incense before them. Oh, for the power of the Holy Spirit to open the eyes, and break the hearts of these poor devil-deluded people. Nothing but this will do in China. If we missionaries are not filled with the Holy Spirit we are worse than useless in China. The devil is exalted here, and, in fact, worshipped. The 'old dragon' is the Chinese national flag, and the dragon is one of their principal gods. Pray for me, Tom, and ask the Lord to fill, and keep me full, of His Holy Spirit.

"I hope you are all well at home. . . . Every day—and sometimes more frequently than once a day

—I mention all your names to the Lord, asking for you all that real love can prompt me to do. Please send me the *Ross-shire Journal* as regularly as you can. It will be nice to see it out here.

"I am not yet certain as to the time when I may start on my long journey for Ta-li-fu. You will doubtless hear again from me ere then. With much love to you all at home, and desiring for you every blessing which our dear Father sees to be good for you, I remain ever your loving brother, in the love of the Lord Jesus.

"WILLIE.

"Psalm xxvii. 1, 2. Give my best love to all the dear young brothers in Dingwall. Ask them to pray for me."

About four months after his arrival in China, and two months before his death, he wrote the following letter :—

"'. . . With us is the Lord our God to help us and to fight our battles.'—2 Chron. xxxii. 8.

"GAN-K'ING, *August 26th, 1882.*

"Dear Mr Broomhall,—Please pardon my seeming negligence in not writing you ere now ; but really time seems to fly so fast in China—a week is gone, and one wonders at its close what he has been doing. The principal part of my time being taken up with the study of the language may, to a certain extent, account for this, as, with the exception of our own special services on the Lord's day, there is nothing in the world around us to mark the flight of time. There is no Sabbath-day in China, although I often think *that* is not true, and the better way, it seems to me, is to say we have Sabbath-days in China, but the Chinese do not keep them. This I know, everything seems different to me on the Lord's day; hill and valley, river and plain—aye, all nature seems on that day to unite in a general song of praise to Him, in whom, and of whom, and by whom are all things, and he alone is silent whose voice ought to lead the anthems of creation. Strange it seems that he who alone was created in the image of his Maker should be the *only* work of His hands in this beautiful world upon which the eye cannot rest with pleasure or the mind dwell without sad thoughts of a dread future. Oh! what hath sin wrought—what misery, what wretchedness, what sorrow, what darkness!

"I do not know to what extent friends at home realise the awful condition of the heathen, but this I do know, that my ideas at home concerning the state of the Chinese came far short of the reality. It is often said by some at home that missionaries, when pleading for the heathen, in their warmth and zeal often exaggerate the condition of the people. Such a thing may or may not have occurred, I cannot say, but I do not think they were missionaries to China. Looking at things as I do, and feeling as I do, it seems to me that that man must be possessed of a most ingenious and imaginative mind who could exaggerate the horrors of 'idolatry,' or the degraded state into which it has brought this mighty nation. Ah, it is impossible to overstate the blessedness of the people whose God is the Lord.

> "'Happy beyond description he
> *Who knows* the Saviour died for *me*.'

"It is equally true that it is impossible to describe the wretchedness of the people whose gods are wood and clay. I have felt during the last fortnight as if I had been living hard by the gates of hell; as soon as I awake in the morning my ears are assailed with the noise of fireworks being let off, the beating of gongs is heard on every side, while cymbals and other like instruments add to the general din. Upon rising and looking out of my windows, the first things my eyes rest upon are the three-cornered paper flags flying from almost every house and shop in the city; these flags are all written over with prayers or the names of the gods. Opening my windows to admit the air, I am almost sickened with the heavy smell of burning incense. I go out, and lo! the idols are set on every hand; opposite the temple of the 'god of rain' a large crowd is gathered, and chairs are constantly arriving and departing with mandarins who have come to pray for rain. A fast has been proclaimed, and only certain kinds of food can be had. All this has been going on during the last fortnight, and will go on, I suppose, increasing in earnestness, until rain comes to refresh the dry and thirsty ground. Now, can one help feeling horrified at all this?

"We, too, are praying unto Him who is the only Hearer and Answerer of prayer, who maketh His sun to rise upon the evil and the good, and sendeth rain on the just and on the unjust. As an evidence of the need of rain in this place, I may say that rice has almost doubled in price since last week; however, from the appearance of the sky to-night, I think we shall have rain before morning.

"And now with regard to myself. I know you will be glad to learn that the Lord continues to help and bless me, and (I trust) to make me a blessing. The summer has been, and still is, a trying one : four times I have been off study for more than a week, and on several occasions for a day or two ; this has been very trying to me, as I am anxious to get on with the language. Oh ! the devil has been making desperate efforts to hinder me—aye, and to discourage me ; but —oh, bless the Lord !—all his efforts have been in vain, for I never was happier than I am just now, never realised the presence of the Lord Jesus more fully than I do now. Glory to His dear name ! I mean to live to please Him. May God help me to do so more and more, for Jesus' sake.

"You will be glad to hear that after quite two years of prayer (I may say, more) the Lord is going to give me the desire of my heart, and send me to Kuang-se, to carry the light of the Gospel to that, at present, dark province. I used to pray specially for this province before offering myself for work in China, and afterwards I changed the 'Lord, send *some one* to Kuang-se,' to 'Lord, send *me* to Kuang-se.' This the Lord has now assured me He is going to do, thus answering both prayers. I really cannot tell with what joy I look forward to the time when I shall be able to go. Since coming to China I have been told what kind of reception I may expect to get at Kuang-se, and have also learned that there are several reasons which, humanly speaking, make the opening of work in that province both difficult and dangerous. This may be so ; but, Mr. Broomhall, I do believe the Lord is going to astonish His servants by the way in which He will open Kuang-se.

"Continue to pray for me, asking the Lord to prepare me for all He is preparing for me ; also please ask the

Lord to prepare the hearts of the people to receive His Word. In this way, if God's people at home, whose hearts have been touched with sympathy for these perishing souls, were to unite in sincere, fervent, and persevering prayer, a great work might be done in Kuang-se before the missionary's voice is heard there. You can easily understand, after this, how I felt on reading the account of the annual meeting; and Mr. Taylor has since informed me that much interest has been raised in behalf of Kuang-se, and I trust this will be followed by earnest, believing prayer."

(To his Parents.)

"GAN-K'ING, *Sep. 12th, 1882.*

"My very dear Parents,—As the mail leaves here to-day, I just take the opportunity of sending you a few lines as I know how welcome a letter from '*Willie*' will be at 3 Albert Place. I hope you are all well at home. I believe were it not that I have left you all in *our Father's* hand I could not bear the thoughts which sometimes force themselves upon me when thinking of you all as so very far away, on the other side of the globe. And yet we are not so very far apart, for you may often reckon on my spirit being with you. Often when at night I stand gazing up at the heavens, and watching the beautiful moon and stars, I think of the beautiful starry nights on which I had done the same thing in far-away Scotland. Then I think of you all, and I believe often when you are perhaps sitting and talking of me I am not so far away as you may think! And yet there is something, oh, so much better, and so much more blessed than this, that He by whom those stars were created, and by whose power they now consist, is always with you, aye, and always with me! It is so blessed to know this. Life without this would to me, in China, be unsupportable. . . . My prayer daily for both of you, my dear parents, is that you would, in an ever-increasing degree, realize this glorious fact, and that the Lord Jesus may be to you an every-day companion, an ever-present, loving, living, bright, glorious reality.

"You will rejoice to hear that when this leaves me I am feeling better in health than I have done for months. . . . The Lord has all along been, oh, so good to me.

"I am still working away at the language. It is a tremendous undertaking. This I am finding out more and more as I go on; and knowing what I now do of it, upon no consideration whatever would I begin the study of it were it not for the object in view, viz., that of telling in their own tongue to millions of heathens the wonderful love of God to me. Not for interest nor for name, would I ever attempt it—

"ONLY FOR JESUS

—but for Him I rejoice to do it, I know He helps me, and long before you get this letter I hope to be able to take prayers with the native Christian teachers. I find I can now fairly well understand the language when it is preached in by any of the missionaries; and I am also able to talk a little with the natives themselves. They all tell me I have very quickly got hold of the sounds and tones. As yet, however, I have only touched the margin of what seems to me a great and almost boundless ocean. You can form no idea of what a strange language Chinese is. It is very rich and expressive, but it has been prostituted to low uses. I shall give you an example or two. . . .

"Oh, do, for Jesus' sake, pray for us in China. We live amongst a people who hate us bitterly, and also hate our teaching, whose favourite name for us, hundreds of times in a day is, 'Foreign Devil!' . . .

"I intended sending Tom a long letter by this mail, but I must be excused. I shall send it by English mail next week if I can get it to the coast. I asked you some time ago to send me the *Ross-shire Journal* as often as you can. You cannot understand how news from a far country cheers, interests, and helps lonely toilers in this dark strange land. . . .

"Pray for "WILLIE."

The above letter occupied 12 8vo. pages of closely written matter.

(His last letter.)

"GAN-K'ING, *September 18th, 1882.*

"My very dear brother Tom,—You have no doubt been expecting word from me ere now. I gladly send you a few lines, and they must of necessity be few, as to-day I am not at all well or strong; and the mail leaves here in an hour and a-half. So again I must please ask to be excused from sending a long epistle. You have no idea, Tom, how close an application to study is necessary if one would make any progress in this most difficult language. Just now, while I snatch time for writing you my head seems so confused, and I am almost writing Chinese. Of course there is no one forcing me to study; there is no one to say 'Yes' or 'No' to me, even if I neglected it all day. But you know that would not do, and I think you can understand how I long to be able to preach Jesus to the poor, wretched, sinful, dying souls around me! So I stick to study as far as health and opportunity will permit me. My attempts at speaking have, with little exception, been confined to my teacher and servant, but I hope to begin this week taking evening prayers with the Christians. Pray for me, dear Tom, that I may be strengthened and helped in acquiring a thorough knowledge of this wonderful language.

"Please not to show hastily written notes such as this to any one, and I shall *(D.V.)* yet send you letters less hurriedly written. Thanks for your hints on acquiring the language, and in another letter I shall tell you to what extent such a style is practicable. Chinese differs so much from all other languages. For instance, besides the numerals employed, as 'one table,' 'one man,' 'one door,' 'one horse,' 'one handkerchief,' in Chinese you use a 'classifier' for each class of things, and if you happen to go wrong in the classification, you will not be understood. I give you the above mentioned articles in Chinese in the same order. They are . . . Each syllable also must have its proper tone and aspirate, or it becomes a different word, and sometimes the learner is very long in the country before he can distinguish some of the differences. Then the *idiom* is also most extraordinary, and as there is no grammar you have no definite rules to go by. The teachers can tell you such is the idiom in this sentence, and so-and-so in the other, but why the difference they do not know, nor does anybody else, so far as I can learn. I could make you laugh if I were to tell you some of our mistakes in this way; but yet it is wonderful how God does help us and enable us to acquire a knowledge of the language.

"The hottest weather is now past for one season, and I may say I am now over my first summer in China. Praise God!

"I have, as you see, not yet started for the far interior, but I suppose ere you receive this note I shall be far from here. But it matters not, Tom, where we are if the Lord Jesus is with us, and if we are where He would have us be.

"I see, however, I must conclude as the brother who is to take my letters is sitting beside me, waiting to go to preach. So please give my best love to dear father, mother, Annie, Jo, and dear Davie, and much love to yourself, dear Tom, from your very loving brother

"WILLIE.

"P.S.—Tom, keep close to Jesus. Whatever others do or say be you out-and-out, whole-hearted, and for our dear Master. He is worthy of all our love—*all* our love mind—*all our love*, Tom.

"WILLIE."

CHAPTER XIV.

HOME.

GOING IN TO SEE THE KING—ILLNESS—PATIENTLY ENDURING THE WILL OF THE LORD—DEPARTING CONSCIOUSNESS—KNOWING JESUS, AND POINTING TO THE SKIES—THE NAME OF JESUS—TESTIMONIES BY FELLOW-MISSIONARIES—THE FUNERAL—LETTER FROM NATIVE TEACHER—LETTER FROM MR. PROTHERO—TESTIMONY BY MR. BROOMHALL.

"I HAVE, as you see, not yet started for the far interior; but, I suppose, ere you receive this note, I shall be far from here."

These words were prophetic in a different and higher sense than the writer of them was aware. Ere the letter reached his much-loved brother, Macgregor had, as he himself phrased it in the case of one of his companions, "*gone in to see the King*" (p. 47). His eyes were beholding the King he served so devotedly, and he was an inhabitant of "the land that is very far off." "But it matters not, Tom, where we are if the Lord Jesus is with us, and if we are where he would have us be." His heart's desire was to be "*with Jesus*" in service in the vineyard; the Master's desire was that he should be with Himself in glory—"Father, I will that they also, whom Thou hast given Me, be with Me where I am; that they may behold My glory, which Thou hast given Me."

"Willie" Macgregor now laid his pen down for the last time. The sequel is told by the loving hands of fellow-missionaries:—

(From Mr. Thomas Prothero, to Tom.)

"INLAND MISSION, GAN-K'ING, CHINA,
Oct. 19th, 1882.

My dear Sir,—Your brother William has asked me to write you a few lines for him, he himself being too unwell to do so at present. For some time he has been the prominent one in nursing our Brother Cooper, but since the two doctors, Messrs Wilson and Edwards, have been here, he himself has been rather unwell, and last Sunday he was ordered by the doctor to go to bed, as he felt so poorly. The doctors watched the symptoms as they manifested themselves, and on Tuesday they said he would be ill for some time. Macgregor has wished me not to let you know what it is he is suffering from, but after some thought I have considered it best to tell you the nature of his disease, as having a knowledge of it you will be the better able to pray for him. You will please not let the knowledge cause you extreme grief. . . . May I urge you to come to our Saviour with this heavy burden, and hear Him—Jesus our Saviour, Jesus the Almighty God, say—'I will give you rest;' 'Casting all your care upon Him, for He careth for you.' The doctors cannot at present say whether the attack will be light or heavy. Do not be alarmed now when I mention that his illness is an attack of small-pox. He has good medical attendance, Dr Wilson himself acting as nurse. Then, too, as to food and medicine, we have all that is necessary, and everything he needs is prepared by two of our lady missionaries at the North Gate, and sent to us here twice a day. There is no lack of anything, and we are well supplied with milk and all that he is likely to need. . . . We rejoice because we trust in a living God, in a God who has in answer to our prayers restored to a very good degree of health our Brother Cooper; and our hope for your dear brother is in the same God. We are in faith praying to God, and we trust Mr. Macgregor will be restored to perfect health, and will soon be standing in China as a herald of Christ's salvation.

"Praying our God to comfort your honoured and aged parents in this time of trial, also to comfort yourself and brother and sisters.—Believe me, dear Sir, to remain the loving friend of your dear brother William; also yours very respectfully,

"THOS. PROTHERO."

Another says that when Macgregor was first informed of the nature of his trouble, his reply was, "I want patiently to endure the will of the Lord."

Dr. Wilson, in a letter written while he was attending Macgregor says: "Last night I was reading over my choice collection of poems, hymns, texts, *etc.*, the valued reminder of so many at home. I have read many to him, and rejoice to find he is one who enjoys

'Ministry of Song,' and other of Miss Havergal's writings. His is a beautifully chastened, quiet Christian spirit, which is the more interesting to me since he told me that before his conversion he was an avowed infidel (or rather Deist). . . .

"If he should be taken, and his missionary career thus be cut off before fairly begun, I feel how appropriate are these lines—I don't know whose they are, but came across them in reading 'Stephen Grellett'—

"'No service in itself is small,
None great, though earth it fill;
But that is small, which seeks its own,
And great which seeks God's will.'"

(From Mr. Prothero to Tom.)

"China Inland Mission, Gan-K'ing,
November 1, 1882.

"My dear Sir,—It is with much sorrow that I write this letter to you. I was hoping when last I wrote that this letter would convey to you tidings of further improvement in your dear brother William. But I am sorry to say that the somewhat favourable symptoms we observed up to Thursday, October 26th, changed later in the day to something of a more serious nature. Later on in the evening Dr. Wilson, who had been watching very closely during the day, came into my room and told me of these more severe and dangerous signs, adding that he feared the worst. Soon after this on the same evening your dear brother became unconscious and remained so, with the exception of two or three intervals, till he died. The night passed with no further signs of any kind, but on Friday morning, October 27, Dr Wilson seemed to be less hopeful of your dear brother's recovery, saying, humanly speaking, and so far as medical skill was of avail, all hope was gone. At Dr. Wilson's suggestion I wrote to our brethren and sisters at the North Gate, telling them how ill he was, and asking them to pray specially for him. We all very dearly loved dear Macgregor, and several times each day did we pray that our Father would, if it were His will, restore one so dear to us to full health. Later on in the evening of Friday, we went in, as we often did, to see him; he seemed to get much worse, and Dr. Wilson sat with him all night. Early on Saturday morning Dr. Edwards and I went to see how he then was. The report was, 'Still the same.' In the evening he seemed to be so very ill that we determined to sit up and to render any help that might be needed. The night passed, and early on Sunday morning dear Macgregor seemed to become more conscious. From Thursday night till Sunday he had known but one person. Drs. Edwards and Wilson asked him several times if he knew them; he shook his head in the negative. Dr. Edwards asked him if he knew JESUS. To this he always nodded his head in the affirmative. Later in the morning of Sunday he seemed to become rather more conscious. Dr Wilson asked him if he knew him, and he nodded his head in the affirmative, also with his right hand, being unable to speak, he wrote the word 'Wilson' on the palm of the left hand. For this sign of consciousness we were thankful, and again became hopeful for his recovery. But he was soon to be gone. The rest of Sabbath passed, his breathing being very fast—sixty to the minute—but he was quieter, and taking a little nourishment. After tea in the evening Drs. Wilson and

Edwards, and I had a prayer meeting for him and others in China, in the room adjoining his, and we seemed to think he would be spared. Dr. Edwards and I retired to our room, intending to revisit your dear brother again before we finally retired.

"Just before this Dr. Wilson again asked him if he knew him. He made signs in the negative, and the Dr. then asked him if he knew—JESUS. He seemed to have no strength to respond by nodding his head, but, as if he knew he was going home, he responded *by lifting his right hand and pointing to the skies.* This was the last sign he gave us.

"That he was going seemed to be deeply impressed upon his own mind. He was often saying 'he thought he was going home.' Dr. Wilson tried to encourage hope in him, but he still thought he was 'going home.' And such was the truth.

"About one o'clock on Monday morning, Dr. Wilson called us and we were soon by his side, just to see him, apparently without a struggle, depart 'to be with Christ, which is far better.'

"Thus did your dear brother William change mortality for life in a brighter and better world. The time in England would be about a quarter to six of Sabbath, Oct. 29th, 1882.

"I cannot write how fully we sympathise with you and your dear parents, and brother and sisters, in this severe affliction. We shall be praying for you all, asking our God, the God of all consolation, to comfort you under this severe trial. Your dear brother William is 'not lost, but gone before,' 'with Christ, which is far better.' We shall follow on.

"I find it impossible to tell you how he was beloved by us. We all loved him. I have just received a note from the Chief Pastor here. He will be writing soon; he asks me to tell you how he—your dear brother,—was loved by us all. He was indeed to us a beloved brother in the Lord, a dear Christian friend. His life was the embodiment of one phrase—that is, *living for Jesus*. . . ."

The mention of the name of JESUS rallied the dying young missionary back to consciousness, as it had often done in the case of others, when everything else had failed. It was a name Macgregor dearly loved. On the cover of his Bible he had pasted the two little pieces given below:—

"JESUS.

"When I can scarcely read or pray,
When troubled thoughts my soul dismay,
His precious name I softly say:
Jesus! Jesus!

"Oh, swifter than a mother's ear,
Her infant's feeble cry to hear,
Is His to catch the trembling prayer:
Jesus! Jesus!

"When sins committed long ago,
Cause bitter tears to flow,
One thought alone can calm our woe:
Jesus! Jesus!

"If sorrow, like a thunder cloud,
In darkest night my soul enshroud,
Out of the depths I cry aloud:
Jesus! Jesus!

"If like a flood the foe come in,
With thoughts of unbelief and sin,
His mighty name the fight shall win:
Jesus! Jesus!

"If worn by long-continued pain,
I sigh for rest and sleep in vain,
Weary, I breathe this prayer again:
Jesus! Jesus!

"*Oh, let His precious name be said*
In whispers o'er my dying bed,
So shall my soul be comforted:
Jesus! Jesus!

"And when upon the other shore
We sin and sorrow nevermore,
His praise shall echo o'er and o'er:
Jesus! Jesus! Jesus!"

WHO LOVED ME—GALATIANS II. 20.

"Three little sunbeams, gilding all I see,
Three little chords, each full of melody,
Three little leaves, balm for my agony.

"'WHO.'

"*He* loved me—the Father's only Son;
He gave Himself, the precious spotless One;
He shed His blood, and thus the work was done.

"'LOVED.'

"He *loved*, not merely pitied: here I rest—
Sorrow may come—I to His heart am pressed;
What shall I fear when sheltered on His breast.

"'ME.'

"Wonder of wonders! Jesus loved ME,
A wretch—lost, ruined, sunk in misery;
He sought me, found me, raised me, set me free.

"My soul the order of the words approve;
Christ first—me last nothing between but love;
Lord, keep *me* always *down*—Thyself *above*.

"Trusting to Thee—not struggling restlessly;
So shall I daily gain the victory;
I, yet not I, but Christ,—'*Who loved me.*'—H. W."

The following letters from fellow-missionaries, who witnessed the closing scenes in Macgregor's life, will be read with interest. They show how he endeared himself to everyone, and afford graphic glimpses of the manner and spirit in which the little bands of God's ambassadors live and love in the heart of a dark and unsympathetic heathendom :—

Miss Southall writes :—"You will doubtless already have heard of the sorrow we have passed through in the removal of our beloved brother, Mr. Macgregor : few, indeed, have I met with who seemed more meet for an inheritance above ; his whole soul was on fire with love to our Saviour, and in his measure I believe it was truly his meat and drink to do His will. We all felt him to be a brother beloved in Christ, and in the power of his godly life he still lives among us."

(From Miss Hughes, to Mrs. Macgregor.)

"CHINA INLAND MISSION, GANG-K'ING,
January 5th, 1883.

"Dear Mrs Macgregor,—Most likely you will be surprised to see the handwriting of a stranger, but Mr Taylor, when here, requested me to write for him, and tell you what I know of your dear son, now in the presence of the Saviour he so devotedly loved on earth. . . . . His life amongst us was so *holy and happy.* The one opinion of everyone is, that he 'walked with God.'

"We used to have, on Sunday nights, English

meetings amongst ourselves. The last time he spoke was from these words, Acts vi. 4, "But we will give ourselves continually to prayer and to the ministry of the Word." So earnest was he: I remember it so well.

"In September Mr Cooper was taken ill; Mr Cooper and he were like brothers, and loved each other intensely. Our dear departed brother nursed him night and day. . . .

"About a fortnight before he (Macgregor) took to his bed he was often poorly. The Saturday he took to bed he complained greatly of thirst. During the evening he sang through and through the hymn,

"'I'm a pilgrim and a stranger.'

"About 9 in the evening I came home; next day (Sabbath) I went to see him, but the fever was high, and his head ached. I sat down by his side and changed the vinegar cloths that the doctors had given him. He told me he was *so happy!* His Heavenly Father was so good to him, that now that he was ill it was nice he was at home with kind friends to care for him. I got him all the things I could to make him comfortable. On Monday afternoon, while the doctors were out I attended to him, and again he said how happy he was, but he was too ill to converse with me. He just asked me to pray for him, and then I left, *little thinking* that in this world I should not gaze again upon that loved face.

"Next day they saw what his trouble was, and so Mr Cooper was moved over here. . . .

"At last Dr Wilson wrote over, telling us that there was no hope of Mr Macgregor—news which bowed us down with grief. We spent nearly the whole day, praying, if consistent with God's will, to spare his life.

"With Saturday came the news 'Nothing is wanted to-day.' All day Sabbath was spent in suspense, and I then quietly hinted to Mr Cooper the serious illness of his loved brother, for he was so ill that we were afraid to let him know.

"On Monday morning, Mrs Tomalin came over and when I saw her face I knew that our beloved brother was with Jesus. . . .

"In the evening we made a wreath, and sent it to be placed on the coffin with the text 'Blessed are the dead who die in the Lord.'

"On Thursday he was buried. Mr Tomalin read the funeral service. . . . He is laid in a pretty, quiet spot, out in the country. We intend planting trees there in the spring. . . .

"We are quite sure the Lord Jesus saw him so ready for Heaven that He longed to have our brother with Himself. Mr Taylor loved him so much, and so did everybody. . . .

"I send you a piece of poetry he liked very much, and which Dr Wilson used to repeat to him. . . .

"May this thought comfort you in the loss of your dear son: it will not be long, and you *will meet him again.* May it not comfort his loved parents, and his young brother whom he so often spoke of, and his two sisters whom he loved so well. Oh! what a joyful meeting that will be—so real and far more joyous than an earthly meeting could be. . . .

"Mr Taylor thought it would comfort you to know

that he not only had a doctor's skill, but all the attention a sister could render him.

"KATIE HUGHES."

Miss Hughes, in sending a translation of a letter of sympathy by Mr. Macgregor's native teacher, says the mutual love of teacher and pupil was very strong. "Often," she says, "when speaking of Mr Macgregor, the tears comes to his eyes."

(The Translated Letter.)

"Dear Mrs Macgregor,—May God protect you, give you happiness, and old age, and constant peace. I belong to China; my name is Cu Fei-Tong, and I wish to tell you, respected parents, that your son's Chinese name was Muh Cï-Kia, or the 'peaceful one.' He last year arrived in China, and came to this city, of Gan-K'ing, to learn to read, and learnt for six months. Every day before he read he first, before me, prayed for God's help in learning the language. He was a very good man. I loved him, and he loved me. I did not think he would take the disease of small-pox, but God wanted him, and, though the body is buried here, his soul is in Heaven. He had several friends to nurse him, nevertheless God wanted him, and he listened.

"I pray you, his respected parents, do not weep; his work is finished. He has obtained his reward in Heaven, and when the Heavenly Father calls you, he will come and meet you and us. I have purposely written this, because I truly loved him.

"CU FEI-TONG, PAI."

Miss Hughes adds that, in his fatal illness, Macgregor was nursed day and night by Dr. Wilson, who could not have shown more Christian and brotherly kindness than he did.

(From Mr Prothero to Tom.)

"West Gate, Gan-K'ing,
November 9th, 1882.

My dear Sir,—You will doubtless be waiting anxiously for a letter concerning your brother William's funeral. The Cemetery we have purchased is a little more than a mile from our Chapel at North Gate. Your brother was buried there in a new grave, at the south end of the Cemetery last Friday, the 3rd inst. The preparations for the funeral were made by Dr Edwards and myself, and out of love for my late dear friend, your brother Willie, we saw that everything needful was not only done, but done by ourselves.

"It will not be needful for me to let you know the particulars, except those of the service. There were present at the funeral service, the Rev. E. Tomalin, who conducted the service in Chinese, also Mrs. Tomalin, Miss Findlay, Miss Evans, Dr. Edwards and I, besides a goodly number of Chinese. After the Chinese service was concluded we sang a hymn from the Wesleyan Methodists' Hymn Book, No. 941. . . ."

A tombstone, erected by his fellow-missionaries, marks the spot where the mortal remains of Macgregor rest till the resurrection morning. The inscription is in Chinese, of which the following is a translation;—

"British Missionary,

"W. M. MACGREGOR.

"Died, October 29th, 1882.

"'Blessed are the dead which die in the Lord from henceforth: yea, saith the Spirit, that they may rest from their labours; and their works do follow them.'

"This stone was erected by his fellow-missionaries in Gan-K'ing."

This Memoir of William Macgregor may be fitly closed with the following appropriate sentences from the pen of Mr Broomhall, Secretary to the China Inland Mission :—

"As we think of the solemn joy with which our brother Macgregor went forth to China; of his manly courage, combined with so much gentleness; of his earnest zeal and great prudence, his tact and kindness, his remarkable power to gain the respect and confidence of those with whom he had to do, we feel that he possessed in no common measure the qualifications for the difficult work of missionary labour in the unevangelised province of Kuang-se. Upon this his heart was set, and his removal does seem a mysterious providence. We cannot explain it; China can ill spare such a man, but in our sorrow we comfort ourselves with the remembrance that the Lord reigns. He can make the removal of our brother a voice to every member of the Mission, calling to renewed consecration to the one work of saving souls from death. He can inspire them with fresh determination to redeem the time and to work while it is day. He can enable each one, with a deeper earnestness than ever, to say, in the words which were our departed brother's last text—'We will give ourselves continually to prayer, and to the ministry of the Word,' and great and blessed results may follow. He can further use our brother's removal to fix the attention of many a young man on the needs of China, and especially of the province to which he had so much desired to go. Many may be baptized for the dead, and desire to take up the work from which he has been called. From such we shall be glad to hear.

"To all, whether at home or in the foreign field, the early removal of our brother speaks with a solemn voice —'WHATSOEVER THY HAND FINDETH TO DO, DO IT WITH THY MIGHT.'"

CHAPTER XV.

ANSWERED PRAYERS.

TRIUMPHANT DEATHS OF FATHER AND ANNIE—ILLNESS OF TOM—EXTRACTS FROM TOM'S LETTERS—CHRISTIAN FORTITUDE AND RESIGNATION IN SUFFERING—A PENSIVE EFFUSION—INTIMATING SERIOUSNESS OF ILLNESS TO THE SUFFERER—POSTHUMOUS LETTER TO FORMER COMPANIONS—SEVENTY-TIMES SEVENFOLD FORGIVENESS—LONGING TO GO HOME—TRIUMPHING IN THE HOUR OF DEATH—LEGACIES OF COMFORT TO FRIENDS—CONVERSION AND DEATH OF JOHANNAH—CLOSING REMARKS.

PRECEDING pages have shown that Macgregor was a man of fervent and importunate prayer. A closing chapter may be profitably devoted to the consideration of the manner and degree in which God graciously vouchsafed answers to his prayers on behalf of those members of the family who have already finished their earthly career. Of the surviving members of the family, for whom Macgregor prayed so earnestly, it would be obviously out of place to speak particularly, further than to say that they are sharers of the same hope with those who have gone before.

The aged father, the elder sister Annie, the younger

brother Tom, and, lastly, the younger sister "Jo," have all been called away in strangely rapid succession, and their bodies repose in Highgate Cemetery, London, in the sure hope of a blessed resurrection. The closing scenes in the life of Tom particularly call for attention, and the remaining pages are mainly devoted to the narration of these.

The family removed from Dingwall, to London, in May, 1883, and shortly afterwards old Mr. Macgregor fell asleep, testifying, even in the last hours of extreme weakness, to the sustaining power and full sufficiency of the grace of God.

Following the death of Mr. Macgregor, "ANNIE"—not long married—died on January 13, 1885. Her dying testimony was bright and reassuring. A few minutes before her end, and, conscious that she was nearing home, she gave each of her sorrowing relatives round her bedside a farewell kiss. Her last words were words of prayer. They were—"Take me! take me! take me!" On the previous night a companion called to see her, to whom she said solemnly—"M——, if you were in my place, would you be prepared to die? If not, be ready!"

On the 21st September following, the specially loved brother, "TOM," was also called away, in the 22nd year of his age. Never robust, his last illness was very protracted. It was brought on by an injury to his knee, occasioned by a fall on the pavement, on the 26th of January, 1885, while going up Old Broad Street, to his business (that of a chemist) in the city. For a long time he hovered, on the borderland, the fluctuations in his health sometimes encouraging hopes of recovery, but extreme weakness invariably intervening and bringing the gentle, patient sufferer down to the verge of death.

Before coming to the closing scene, however, extracts from two of his letters will indicate his spiritual state while still in comparative health. To the friend who led him to Christ (pp. 71-74) he wrote, shortly after reaching London—

"I must say that never before have I felt as I do now, the necessity of leaning on Christ for help to fight the battle of life. I never before felt how sweet it is, amid the surrounding loneliness, to have such a Friend as the Lord Jesus to commune with, as I pass through wildernesses of unknown faces. Truly God has fulfilled the promise to me, 'My grace is sufficient for thee!' I left Dingwall very weak in body, and not very bright in spirits, and, lo, contrary to my anticipations, He has preserved me on my journey, and continues to restore my bodily vigour. When I was a week or two here I tried for a situation, and laid the matter before the Lord, and He gave me my choice of several places. . . . I accepted the one nearest home, which also was the one with the shortest hours, and which, of course, was the one that suited me best. . . .

"You deserve well of me because you showed yourself a true friend. In fact, at a time when I despised you, you were praying for me, and seeking my salvation."

On November 15, 1884, he wrote—

"It seems rather hard that as we grow up we have to part company with one another, perhaps for life. However, we shall have plenty time up yonder to talk over these matters. . . .

"Since your last letter one more tie binding me to earth has been loosed, and there is one more tie binding me to Heaven. I did not think I should miss my dear father as I do. Scarcely a night passes but I dream of him. We all miss him very much. '*Till the heavens be no more, he shall not arise nor awake out of his sleep.*' That verse comforted me at Willie's death—'*Till the heavens be no more.*"

On the 26th of January, 1885, as already mentioned, the shock to his already enfeebled system, brought on complete prostration, and a long period of intense suffering. The pain for a time was so severe that he could not bear, without shrinking, that anyone should touch his bed, but he bravely strove against a murmuring spirit. The intensity of the pain gradually abated, only to give place, however, to another form of trial, which, in its way, was equally difficult to bear. Possessing a keen intellect of remarkable power, he had carefully prepared for examination with a view to obtaining a Science and Art Scholarship, in South Kensington, tenable for three sessions, and genorously granted by H. M. Matheson, Esq., of Hampstead, to the Dingwall Science Classes, of which Tom was for several years the leading student. The poor lad coveted, more than anything else of a temporal character, this Scholarship, with its congenial and extended course of study in scientific subjects. When at last everything was ready, and it was arranged that he could take his examination papers in London, his kind medical adviser—Dr. Keele—perceiving the serious nature of his disorder, forbade him absolutely from entertaining the prospect so dear to him. In a letter, intimating this decision, on April 13th, Tom says he was then still in bed, unable to put his foot under him. It was at this time he wrote the pensive lines given below :—

"I' e gazed upon these walls so long,
That they have quite familiar grown,
And like some old, endearing song
Each line and syllable is known.

"Or like a vale, where rivers wend,
O'er plains of pink to seas of blue,
While round the land the coast-lines stand,
And hills, like feathers, lie in darker hue;

"While over all the names are spread
Of countries, cities, isles, and seas—
So on the wall beside my bed
Each spot familiar is as these.

"Here have I lain since winter's breath
Chilled the damp street with hazy gloom;
Sweet snowdrops nodding over death
Spake of white robes beyond the tomb.

"The winter waned, and welcome spring
Spread the fair plains with opening flowers;
The southern birds on hasty wing,
Sped to their decorated bowers,

"Filling the trembling air with song:
But yet to me no spring appears,
Nor summer day so bright and long,
Smiling, my drooping spirit cheers.

"Though on no summer fields I gaze,
A land of joy is full in sight;
My heart is full of peace and praise:
The Lord's my Sun, the Lamb's my Light.

"Here with my Saviour I am blest,
No other pleasure half so sweet;
His angels guard His humble guest,
And slow-winged hours seem almost fleet.

"'Tis better thus with soul at rest,
While here the aching flesh remains,
Than roam the earth with troubled breast,
The body free, the soul in chains."

Mr. W. C. East, secretary of the Shoreditch Branch of the Y.M.C.A., who kindly helped to nurse Tom, supplies an account of his last illness, from which several extracts are made.

"In May," says Mr. East, "by God's goodness in blessing the Dr.'s skill, and with the aid of a crutch, Tom was able to move about the room. By June he was able to take his first walk out of doors, leaning on my arm, supporting himself also on his crutch. We had taken several short walks of this kind, when I had to leave for my holidays. On my return I found that he had broken a small blood vessel, which again prostrated him. He never again rose from his bed. It was a very hot summer, and must have proved very trying to him, but he never murmured. Ice was applied to his head and breast day and night, and he was rarely left alone for an hour, until his death in September following. None, next to his mother, was more assiduous and devoted in nursing than his sister, Johannah—her touch soothed him, and her singing afforded him much delight. In August Dr. Keele told his friends that there was no hope of recovery. One lung had already become consolidated, and the other was seriously affected. It was, after a time, thought best to tell him how near the hour of his departure might be, and I was asked to do so. He received the news very quietly, the only symptom of feeling being a slight flushing of the face. He then said quietly that he was resigned to God's will, and never after spoke of possible recovery, and neither did he speak of 'death.' A week before his end he asked me to write to his dictation a letter to two of his former companions in Dingwall. He was much exercised in prayer as to the spiritual condition of these lads."

It was arranged by the dying lad that the letter, which he signed with his own hand, would not reach its destination till after his death. The letter, which is given below, is at once an assuring and happy deathbed testimony, and a particularly solemn and pathetic appeal to the two young men to decide for Christ. Its publication, in these pages, may affect hearts for which the meek writer never intended it :—

"135 Roman Road, Barnsbury,
London, *31st August, 1885.*

"Dear ——, and ——,—I have a very strong desire to write one more letter before I pass away from earth to Heaven, to plead with you to give your hearts to the Lord Jesus Christ. I am far too ill to write the letter myself, so I get a dear friend to do so for me at my dictation.

"I have on former occasions pleaded with you to turn to Christ Jesus, who is the only Saviour, and through Him alone can you escape from the wrath to come. To me at this time nothing can avail but Christ Jesus.

"Soon, very soon, and before you get this letter, I shall have said the last good-bye to my friends, and have passed to be with my Lord. Think of this, that while *you are* reading this letter, *I am* with Christ, beholding His face, and enjoying the full blessing of Heaven. Oh, would it not have been folly for me to have put off the decision of my soul's salvation till *now?* And could I lie upon my pillow with ease of mind and a desire to depart if I had rejected the Lord's call?

"Oh———, and ———, pray God *at once* to give you His Spirit, and for Christ's sake to pardon your sins. Perhaps soon you may have to leave this world and to stand before God. Can you with ease and quietude of mind anticipate such a thing? 'I pray you in Christ's stead be ye reconciled to God.' 'God is love.' 'He willeth not the death of any, but that all should turn to Him and live.' 'The blood of Jesus Christ, God's Son, cleanseth us from all sin,' and though your sins be as great mountains yet God, for Christ's sake, will forgive you. Turn to God at once. Do not delay. Remember that God hath not promised you another day; but plead with God *now*, and come unto Him.

"Will you read John's Gospel, chapter iii., and the first 21 verses, especially think of verse 16.

"I am with Christ, and I want to meet you there. Oh, do not let me look for you in vain! This is my last word—'God is love.'—Your old companion,

"T. G. MACGREGOR."

Mr East writes:—"At the time of writing to his former companions I had a talk with him concerning his personal trust in Christ, and the clearness of his views in regard to pardon and acceptance. His replies were extremely simple and touching.

"He said—'I have a full belief in Jesus Christ as my personal Saviour. I rest alone upon His Word, and have confidence in the power of His blood to cleanse away my sin.'

"Asked if he had any concern regarding the future, he replied—'There is an exception to my complete restfulness. My sins of omission and commission since my conversion, the knowledge of inconsistency and want of conformity to His holy will, come with force to my heart just now and trouble me.'

"'But, Tom, does not the blood of Jesus Christ cleanse us from *all* sin?'

"'Yes,' was his answer, 'it does, I fully believe, but still I am troubled.'

"'But do you not think this mingling of gall in your cup of joy a potion from the evil one?'

"'It may be so, but my rest is disturbed by it,' he replied.

"I was sorely grieved for my dear friend. It was the first indication of unrest of mind or spirit, and I scarcely knew what to say to dispel the cloud, when suddenly there came to my mind the question of Peter to Jesus, 'Lord, how oft shall my brother sin against me, and I forgive him? Till seven times? Jesus saith unto him, I say not unto thee until seven times, but until seventy times seven' (Matthew xxiii. 21-22). I read these words to him, and added,

"'Do you think, dear Tom, that the Lord Jesus Christ

would teach His disciples to do that which He Himself is not ready to do?'

"His answer was a silent, but inexpressible look of joy. In a moment or two he added,

"'Oh, yes, I see; Jesus will forgive me seventy times-seven times. Oh, how loving! how good!'

'The light of the Saviour's love and compassion broke in afresh upon his soul, and from that moment there was great readiness to depart and be with Christ. Two or three days before the end he clasped his hands together, and prayed with intense fervour,

"'Oh, come Lord Jesus! Come! Make haste!'

"His peace remained calm as a river. On the last night of his illness I relieved his mother at midnight, and sat up with him till five o'clock of the morning."

Mr. East, in detailing the experiences of the closing hours of Tom's life, states that short periods of semi-consciousness occurred several times, in all of which the mind centred on the Saviour he loved so much. A few minutes before his death, which took place at noon, and while his faculties were quite clear, he suddenly burst forth into fervent and importunate prayer that God's name might be glorified everywhere, and ascribing all power and glory to Jesus his Saviour. He then sang, unaided, a Psalm from the Scottish metrical version with great rapture, the vigour with which he engaged in these exercises surprising and over-powering everyone present. Dr. Keele afterwards went to the bedside, and gently called Tom by name. The dying lad, in response, opened his eyes and smiled a happy recognition. He then again lapsed into unconsciousness, and without a quiver fell asleep.

Fully aware that his death would be keenly felt by the loved friends he was leaving behind, Tom sought to console them with the comforts wherewith his own soul was comforted of God. "I know," he said to his mother, "you will miss me, but do not think of me as being dead, for I shall be with Jesus." Towards his end he asked his friend, Mr East, to address separately to his mother and sister and brother, slips of paper written by himself, each containing a text of Scripture, the slips to be retained till after his death. These slips were:—

"*Comfort from the Lord to my darling Mother.*—'But I would not have you to be ignorant, brethren, concerning them which are asleep, that ye sorrow not, even as others which have no hope' (1 Thes. iv. 13)."

"*Comfort from the Lord to my darling sister, Jo.*—'Thy brother shall rise again' (John xi. 23.)"

"*Comfort from the Lord to my darling brother, Davie.*—'Thou, therefore, my son, be strong in the grace that is in Christ Jesus' (2 Tim. ii. i)."

The funeral services were conducted by the Rev. Mr. Sawday, now of Leicester. Besides the relatives, a large number of former fellow-Christian workers assembled, who, before the grave was closed, joined in singing Tom's favourite hymn—

"Jesus, thy blood and righteousness
My beauty are, my glorious dress;
'Midst flaming worlds, in these arrayed,
With joy shall I lift up my head."

The reader must have been impressed with the intensity of William Macgregor's desires and prayers for the conversion of his sister, "Jo." He had the assurance that sooner or later his prayers on her behalf would be answered. The answer, though for a time delayed, came at last. For several years she was in a state of anxiety, more or less deep, regarding her soul; but it was not till the spring of 1884 that she found rest, in the acceptance of Christ as her complete and personal Saviour. Her conversion occurred under the preaching of Mr. D. L. Moody, the American evangelist, in the great iron tent erected at St. Pancras during Mr. Moody's memorable mission to London. In the full zeal of her first love she at once threw herself into Christian work of a kind suited to her talents, such as tract distribution, assisting with the singing at open-air meetings, and dealing with anxious inquirers. Her sky was not always bright, however, for she was often cast down in spirit by a sense of unworthiness, but only to be raised up again by fresh realizations of the worthiness and love of her Redeemer.

"How unworthy I am," she often said; "but, oh, how much Jesus does love me! Oh, how good He is to me!"

After a period of severe and protracted illness, fitted to test the genuineness of her faith in Christ, and in which her chastened spirit bore testimony to God's faithfulness she passed to her rest, to rejoin loved ones "gone before," on the Queen's Jubilee Day, June 21, 1887.

"Come, Lord Jesus, oh, come quickly," was a prayer she more than once uttered during her last night on earth. To the question, put several times during that night, if she were still trusting Jesus, she had but one reply—

"Oh, yes; He is all my salvation, and all my desire."

Her favourite hymn, during her illness was—

"Fade, fade, each earthly joy: Jesus is mine!
Break, ev'ry tender tie; Jesus is mine:
Dark is the wilderness,
Earth has no resting-place;
Jesus alone can bless, Jesus is mine!

"Tempt not my soul away; Jesus is mine!
Here would I ever stay; Jesus is mine!
Perishing things of clay,
Born but for one brief day,
Pass from my heart away! Jesus is mine!

"Farewell, ye dreams of night; Jesus is mine!
Lost in this dawning light; Jesus is mine!
All that my soul has tried
Left but a dismal void;
Jesus has satisfied; Jesus is mine!

"Farewell, mortality; Jesus is mine!
Welcome, eternity; Jesus is mine!
Welcome, O loved and blest,
Welcome, sweet scenes of rest,
Welcome, my Saviour's breast; Jesus is mine!"

William Macgregor's letters and diary, together with the devotion of his life, read out with unwavering decisiveness and holy emphasis their own moral. They show that the "new birth"—a living faith in a crucified and risen Saviour—is the true starting point in spiritual life. They are also calculated both to stimulate desires after whole-hearted, personal consecration, and to teach, in no small measure, the secret of continuous and rapid growth in the Christian life.

They are fitted, likewise, to fire with missionary zeal hearts that have remained indifferent, or become lethargic with regard to the last great command of the Lord Jesus Christ, "Go ye into all the world, and preach the Gospel to every creature" (Mark xvi. 15). "Say what you will about the *needs* of home, and the *claims* of home," said the Rev. Dr. J. H. Wilson, of the Barclay Church, Edinburgh, a few years ago, "the fact is undeniable, that there are comparatively few at home who have not the opportunity, in some way, of knowing as much about Christ as may suffice for their salvation, while *three-fourths of the whole people of the world* are as ignorant of Christ, and of the way of life, as they were that day when the Lord declared His mind so commandingly to Paul." (Acts xxii. 21). Since these striking words were uttered missionary effort has been pushed forward with an amount of enterprise and zeal unprecedented since Apostolic days. The result is, that the number of those who have never heard the Gospel has been reduced from three-fourths to *two-thirds* of the entire population of the world. The progress made is remarkable, for not only has the Word of Life been proclaimed in the ears of thousands for the first time, but statistics show that, if the number of labourers and the amount of means expended are compared, the rate of progress made by Christian Churches planted in heathen countries is much greater than that made by the Churches at home. But the appalling fact remains, that out of the world's population of 1,424,000,000 souls there are 856,000,000 who have never heard the name of Jesus! The odds seem to be overwhelmingly against the Church, but there is no reason for despair. On the contrary, the mission field is now in a more hopeful state than ever it was, and the Churches are awaking, as never before, to the claims of Christ and the heathen. Lady Aberdeen, in an address to young women, delivered in the town of Peterhead some months ago, made a very significant and suggestive statement. It was to this effect. Assuming the population of the world to be what it is, and that there were only *one Christian* amongst those 1,424 millions, if that Christian brought *one soul every year to Christ*, and if all the souls thus brought were instrumental, each in his or her turn, in bringing in others in like manner, in *thirty-three* years the kingdoms of this world would become the kingdoms of our Lord and His Christ. The statement seems scarcely credible, but when tested it will be found quite within the mark. The world for Christ in thirty-three years! The lofty ambition ought to fire every Christian heart. Lady Aberdeen, however, assumed *only one* Christian to begin with, in the world's population. But matters being as they are the suggestion, made in 1886, by the Rev. Dr. Somerville, Moderator of the Free Church of Scotland, *that the world might be evangelised before the close of the century*, was sufficiently modest, if the Church but awoke to a full sense of her duty. The heathen are entitled to expect greater ardour and self-denial in missionary work than anything history has yet recorded.

Mr. Hudson Taylor, in relating some of the hardships he, along with the late Rev. W. C. Burns, experienced during his early days in China, tells the following remarkable incident. After they had spoken one day in the city of Ningpo one of the listening crowd said :—

"I have long sought for the truth ; I and my father before me. I have found no rest in Confucianism, Buddhism, Taoism ; but I do find rest in what I have heard here. Henceforth I believe in Jesus."

Afterwards he asked Mr. Taylor how long the Glad Tidings had been known in England. When he was told,

"Some hundreds of years," he looked amazed.

"What !" he exclaimed, "is it possible, and yet you have only now come to preach them to us ? My father sought after the truth for more than twenty years, and died without finding it. Why did you not come sooner ?"

The reader must have been also struck with Macgregor's intense solicitude for the salvation of the individual members of his family. His earnest personal remonstrances and importunate prayers, it will have been seen, were wonderfully rewarded. No one can be fitted for missionary work abroad, or, indeed, for any form of Christian work, who is indifferent to the salvation of personal friends. That man is likely to be most owned of God who is deeply in earnest about the spiritual state of his own family. And no work is more hopeful. Sanctified natural affections, when wisely and zealously directed, are sooner or later—and oftener soon than late—sure to prove irresistible. But no work depends so much upon the *real* personal life of the Christian, for in family life guises cannot long pass muster. *Families complete in all their memberships in Christ!*—there is a sacred charm in the thought, just as there is unutterable dread in the thought of family separations throughout eternity. The work, too, of winning one's friends for Christ, where the heart and life are right, is the easiest form of work, just as it is the readiest to hand, and needs less qualifications than almost any other. It is a sphere peculiarly suited to young Christians as a "first field of operations," and no seals of accepted ministry in future and wider service will be valued more than when, in the enthusiasm of first love, personal friends are led to the Lord. What the saintly Samuel Rutherford was in the habit of saying to his congregation at Anwoth—"Your salvation would be two salvations to me, and your Heaven would be two Heavens to me"—is a sentiment that might, with even more appropriateness, be entertained by Christian friends in seeking the salvation of members of their own families. If the Life of William Macgregor will stimulate to more prayerful earnestness, and greater exertions in this direction alone, it will not have been published in vain.